My Story
This is
My Song

This is My Story This is My Song

Mary Bramer

Publishing House
St. Louis

Copyright © 1984 Concordia Publishing House
3558 South Jefferson Avenue
St. Louis, Missouri 63118-3968

Printed in the United States of America

Library of Congress Cataloging in Publication Data

Bramer, Mary.
    This is my story, this is my song.

    Summary: The author, paralyzed by polio in high school, relates her experiences, and her determination to go to college and become a school teacher despite her handicap.
    1. Bramer, Mary. 2 Christian biography—United States. 3. Poliomyelitis—Patients—United States—Biography. (1. Bramer, Mary. 2. Poliomyelitis—Patients. 3. Physically handicapped. 4. Teachers. 5. Christian life.) I. Title.
BR1725.B682A37 1984   248.8'6'0924 (b) (92)   83-25176
ISBN 0-570-03923-1

---

1 2 3 4 5 6 7 8 9 10 DB 93 92 91 90 89 88 87 86 85 84

For my parents

No one who reads this book
will ever need to ask why.

Contents

Acknowledgments

Writing this book has not been a solo endeavor. For their earthly help and co-operation, I wish to acknowledge the following:

Doris Monson, Sue Johnson, Russ Ingraham, and other dear friends who gave me such positive encouragement to keep going;

Jewell Lawrence and her Bible class for unfailing support;

Alice H. Mortenson for permission to include her poems and Beacon Hill Press for the lines from "I Needed the Quiet";

John D'Arcy and the Chicago Sunday Evening Club for hours of inspiration and permission to quote from several programs;

Pastor L. W. Schuth for his funeral sermon and, along with Pastor Harold Ross and the other pastors throughout my life, for faithful presentation of the Word;

Fred Schuchert for his help with the song "My Grace";

Bob Schwarzkopf for his photographs and the *Daily Courier News* for permission to use several photographs;

Hope Publishing Company, Carol Stream, IL, for permission to quote from the hymn "Great Is Thy Faithfulness," copyright 1923; renewal 1951. All rights reserved;

Edith and Al Bramer who again did what they have always done and continue to do so well—care.

Introduction

More than 30 years ago illness changed me from an active, strong teenager to a quadriplegic — a cripple with paralysis in all four limbs. To say that this changed my life would be understatement in the extreme. Yet to imply that my life stopped at that point would also be wrong. With the support and dedication of my most wonderful parents, I have had a satisfying life — though in no way similar to the one I had envisioned for myself. My life is not a story of human victory. Rather it is the story of a faithful God being with three of his believers as they passed through the waters.

After the initial stages of my illness, I was left with countless things I could not do. The doctors told my parents all the things I would never be able to do again — walk, run, stand, use my arms and hands, sit upright without bracing, sing, and simple pleasures beyond immediate comprehension. What most of the medical personnel failed to mention was what could be done with scattered traces of muscles, a good mind, devoted parents, and the help of God.

Over the years my mother has encouraged me to write about my life. She and I both have read many books about others who have also been confined to wheelchairs. She has thought that I should make a similar accounting, but it has been difficult for me to speak about my personal life. However, the wishes of a mother like mine should never be ignored. For her I begin this task.

Even with the passage of time and the perspective of maturity, this was not easy. Each time I sang in church or at a wedding, I battled with my butterfly nerves. Whenever I taught a class with a visitor present or spoke to teachers at a meeting, I was nervous. As difficult as those experiences were, it was much harder for me to talk or write about myself. Yet I do have a story I can tell, and I do have praises to

11

sing. Although many of the principals involved in my life are still alive, I did not consult with any of them to confirm my memory or add details. This will be the account of my life as I remember it, as it has been told to me, and as it is recorded in a collection of old letters and papers. This is an account of my family and me as we lived each day with the blessed assurance that God's grace is sufficient. Very simply, this is my story; this is my song.

E'en Though
It Be a Cross

The house held a heavy summer stillness punctuated only by the far-off sounds of children playing or an occasional car passing by. "Fair are the meadows, Fair are the woodlands," I sang through the silent house, my fingers pressing out the simple hymn chords on the piano. "He makes our sorr'wing spirit sing."

People used to say that walking through Carpenter Park a block and a half from her home, they could hear my grandmother singing in her kitchen as she went about her household chores. Later they said that I had inherited my strong voice from Grandma Bramer, although I never remembered hearing her sing. As I had known her, those last years of her life had been burdened with illness and slow healing. Some said I looked like my grandmother, but I saw little resemblance to the young woman with the dark hair in the old brown photograph. Perhaps the resemblance was in my music and love of singing.

My grandfather had been musical, too, but I had never heard him play the accordian either. By the time I knew him, the drop forge he operated had cut off or mutilated several of his fingers. I knew of the accordian in its great dusty case in the upstairs closet and had heard of his playing at street dances. An old photograph showed him holding his beautiful accordian. How calm he had looked sitting in the wicker chair!

I was far from calm. Frequently, when I was alone in the house that summer, I had sought comfort at the piano singing the old hymns. "Take my life and let it be Consecrated, Lord, to Thee; Take my moments and my days. . ." My voice broke from its steady tone as

13

it had so often lately. Unbidden, the tears slipped from my eyes, and my throat tightened. The hymnbook seemed to fall open automatically to the one song that spoke to me that year.

> Nearer, my God, to Thee, Nearer to Thee.
> E'en though it be a cross That raiseth me,
> Still all my song shall be, Nearer, My God, to Thee,
> Nearer, my God, to Thee, Nearer to Thee.

It was a troubled summer. My soul was restless; my inner self dissatisfied. I thought I knew what was coming, for I had had a clear premonition. I knew in the spring of 1949 that I was going to contract polio.

I had glimpsed my own future while watching a movie about infantile paralysis in health class. Near the end of the movie, the young victim was taking labored steps down a long hall, awkwardly managing her little wooden crutches. Her mother appeared, walked toward her, stooped down, and held out her arms. The little girl dropped her crutches and made a clumsy dash to her mother's arms. The thought flashed through my mind that this was one illness to which I hadn't subjected my parents, and I knew with a certainty that I would.

I had taken my parents through a series of crises. I had been operated on six times from ruptured appendix to minor oral surgery. I had had nearly every childhood illness and several of them twice. Since most had occurred before the days of hospitalization insurance, it seemed that every time my parents had a little money saved, I had some illness to empty the bank account again. Yet I was a strong, healthy girl in 1949—tall, slender, still wearing eyeglasses as I had since my second birthday. I led a vigorous life with boundless energy filling physically demanding days.

Like my older brother, I was working, saving money for the college education I wanted. He was enrolled for the fall term at the University of Illinois, having graduated from high school the past June with highest honors in mathematics. His goal was to become a structural engineer. He was working that summer, as he had all throughout high school, for a local florist.

I planned to follow him to the university four years later to pursue a career in either music or fashion design. I was also working full-time that summer—seven and a half hours a day, five days a week—at the public library as a page in the reference department. I was really too young, but the librarian had liked my straight-A report card and my willingness to work. I had been given a raise after the first month from 25 to 30 cents an hour. Babysitting paid better—usually 40 cents an hour with an occasional tip—but it was only for a few hours a couple of nights a week. The library provided steady work and still allowed babysitting several times a week. I felt so grown-up.

14

It was a thrill being a working girl right downtown, window-shopping on my lunch hour. I loved buying some of my own clothes for school, like the red corduroy suit and red plaid blouse I had splurged to get. I carried my lunch to save money and usually walked back and forth to work to save bus fare, too. Occasionally, the oppressive heat of summer in the upstairs of the old library drove me to spend 15 cents in the afternoon for a vanilla coke.

Even though things were going so well, I was subconsciously aware of an elusive discontentment. Perhaps I envied my brother's positive direction, knowing exactly what career he wanted and which school provided the best preparation he could afford. I enjoyed music, both singing and playing the piano, but I lacked the dedication to spend long hours in daily practice. I loved designing clothes, especially shoes, but I had no idea at all how anyone pursued a career in the competitive field of fashion. But I had four years of high school first before I had to make choices, so it really wasn't career uncertainty that bothered me.

I think I knew that the commitment my life lacked was a spiritual direction. I really didn't like the person I was. I was a church member and had attended church and Sunday school all my life. Yet something was very wrong with my relationship to God.

Again and again that summer I found myself at the piano intending to practice but turning instead to the hymnbook. Since my premonition that I would have infantile paralysis, "Nearer, My God, to Thee" had become almost a theme song. I knew subconsciously what the "cross" would be that was to bring me nearer to my God. I told no one, but waited silently for the coming attack of polio.

I quickly read every magazine that came into the library with a story or article on polio—especially the suggestions on how to avoid catching the disease: avoid scant or irregular meals; avoid becoming overtired; avoid crowds; avoid overwork; avoid taking a chill; avoid public beaches.

One noon hour my fellow page and I window-shopped in the downtown area several blocks from the library. A sudden thunder shower caught us, and we stood in a doorway waiting for it to pass.

"I don't think it's going to stop," Lylas offered.

I felt I must not break my record and be late back to work. "Let's make a run for it," I suggested. We ran back trying to stay under awnings as much as possible, but my cotton blouse and skirt were wet when we arrived—on time—back at the library.

I changed my wet blouse for my smock and tied my apron on backwards under my wet skirt. I improvised an apron of paper towels to pin under the front of my skirt. I congratulated myself that I seemed quite dry as long as I remained standing. I walked about the library rustling softly in my paper-towel petticoat. That dampness and clammy feeling couldn't be considered a chill, could it?

A girlfriend invited me to join her and her parents for a day at Lake Geneva on my day off. Swimming and the water seemed to carry a special fear, yet I had been working hard all summer and wanted the relaxation. A family consensus was reached that I could go. The day was perfect with surprisingly few people on the beach. How clever of us to pick that day! We swam and picnicked, and my health seemed so good. There was nothing to that water fear after all, was there?

Our church's 10th anniversary celebration involved us all. A big tent was set up on the vacant lots where someday a new church would be built. I sang in the choir, waited on tables, and soloed in the entertainment. We were all exhausted. Considering the warm weather and my usual problems with hayfever and allergies, I was no more worn out than anyone else. That wasn't being overtired, was it?

One Sunday in mid-August after early church and Sunday school I sat upstairs in my bedroom with the back-to-school fashion section from the *Chicago Tribune*. I was busily sketching and designing when I became aware of a chill. My feet were like ice. I put on my wool skating socks to warm my feet and continued drawing. When dinner was called, I appeared in the hot kitchen wearing wool socks. Mother knew instantly I was sick. Her prescription—bed rest with a blanket.

Dad was leaving the next day by car on a business trip taking my brother with him. There was no need to change that because of my slight fever and chills, but I was definitely not to go to work that Monday. Dad made that an order because I was hard to keep home from work or school unless I was half dead. Tuesday would be my day off. Mother could make the decision about Wednesday depending on how I would be feeling then.

I knew I was going to get polio, but not *when*. Maybe it wouldn't be for years. After all, I could still walk. I was sure this wasn't it—yet!

Jesus Calls Us

Jesus calls us; o'er the tumult
Of our life's wild, restless sea,
Day by day His sweet voice soundeth,
Saying, "Christian, follow Me."

In our joys and in our sorrows,
Days of toil and hours of ease,
Still He calls, in cares and pleasures,
"Christian, love Me more than these."

I can never praise God enough for bringing my parents together to join their lives and establish a Christian home. What an unbeatable combination they have been. They were married in 1928 after a five-year courtship. Mother always claimed that she thought Dad would never propose, so finally in leap year she asked him. She was the youngest of nine children who had reached adulthood; Dad was the older of two. Both were essentially first-generation Americans. Like their parents, they believed in working hard to make life better for the next generation. Dad was a licensed professional engineer working in the city engineer's office and playing saxophone in a small dance band—an extra job he quit when they married. Mother quit her job in the office of the Elgin National Watch Company and used her savings as the down payment on a small home. They were married at Mother's home by the pastor from her church.

By the time I was expected, much in their world had changed. The Depression had come. Four years after they married, my older brother was born. Like millions of others, Dad had a period when he was out of work for several months. The kindness of the president of the loan association that held their mortgage allowed them to save their home. He asked only that they keep up the interest portion when they could not make the full payment for a few months. During those same years both of Mother's parents died. When the second child was expected, they needed a larger house — especially when the second child turned out to be a girl.

Mother and Dad sold their honeymoon cottage for only half of what the paid for it, but they were able to buy a large, comfortable home on a big corner lot at the same depression prices. It was a good family house. I remember that house and neighborhood so well. My brother and I went through the same grade school with nearly the same teachers. Most of the same students were in our classes through all six grades. Few of our neighbors moved in the 16 years we lived there. Life was more stable in those days.

Although I was born during the Depression, I remember nothing of that time. I know that the waived mortgage payments allowed our savings to carry us through. Just when our resources were at their lowest ebb, my father was asked to plot out an addition to a cemetery in his hometown. The $400 he received for his work seemed like $4,000 at the time.

Dad was also a licensed surveyor and was clever and quick to understand complicated mechanical and electrical things. He could repair nearly anything at our home when it broke. He was a good painter, but he never liked to do it. Sometimes his work had to be so perfect to meet his own standards that he was painstakingly slow. He quoted to all of us the same rule he followed himself, "Anything worth doing is worth doing well." He felt there was one right way to do everything.

Dad was musical and had a beautiful baritone voice. I can't remember when we didn't sing together. Even as a little girl I knew and loved the World War I songs he sang. But it was his hobby of photography that I liked best. Many evenings we worked together in the improvised darkroom in our basement. Gently sloshing the prints in the solutions until the images appeared black and sharp was more like play than work.

I found it harder to work for my mother. She was such an efficient, organized homemaker that she didn't need me at all. I also didn't find cleaning, bed-making, and dish-washing very interesting — at home. I would willingly do any of it for my piano teacher, however. Mother was an excellent cook and baker. Her fudge was everybody's favorite. Both my brother and I were expert tasters and bowl-lickers. His specialty was the fudge; mine was raw pie crust and cake dough. Endless donations of food left our house for church suppers and bazaars. It sometimes seemed that more went out than was kept for us. It was not unusual to come home from school and find a freshly frosted cake on the kitchen counter and cookies cooling on brown paper on the kitchen table.

Sonny's first question was always, "Is that for us, or is it going somewhere?"

The answer was often, "The cake is for Aunt Rose's bridge club, and the cookies are going to the bake sale. You can have some cookies though."

Mother had a reputation for hospitality. She often hosted the big family gatherings—holiday meals, Sunday dinners, and summer suppers on the screened front porch. She took a special pride in her reputation as a good manager because she could stretch her food budget to the maximum without being skimpy.

In fact, Mother was a good household manager. If there was a shortage of money, her wants came last. Although my parents planned to replace the furnace in their larger home eventually, the need came sooner than expected. The cost of the new furnace and an automatic stoker was higher than anticipated.

"What's more," Dad said, "we'll have to pay some pick-up service to come and haul the old furnace away."

"Wouldn't somebody want it for the scrap iron?" Mother wondered.

"All right," Dad said, "you find someone who does." So she did. She called the scrap metal dealers listed in the phone book and found one who would come to pick up the furnace. What's more, he paid for the scrap iron. When he arrived, he gave Mother an estimate of the weight before he began removing the pieces.

"I think it would weigh more than that," Mother reasoned. "Iron's heavy. You should know."

"Well, maybe so," the dealer conceded. He must have known he was estimating light because he eventually paid Mother more than twice his original price.

I suppose we were a poor family by today's standards. We never rented a cottage or took a vacation trip. Once during World War II Dad gave up his vacation to make an emergency trip to Florida. As compensation he was allowed to use a company car and take his family along.

We found contentment at home. Our social life was built around the family and church. Shortly after buying their bigger home, my parents became charter members of a new mission congregation. They worked hard building both the membership and the church building. Mother helped organize the ladies' group and taught Sunday school. Dad was a church officer and elder at various times.

World War II came with its rationing and shortages. We saved scrap metal, paper, kitchen grease, and flattened tin cans. We bought savings stamps and war bonds whenever we could and sent packages to friends and relatives in service. Dad was air-raid captain for our block, and we diligently practiced our drills and blackouts.

Metal toys all but disappeared for children because of the war effort. Plastic was not yet common, and cardboard was a poor substitute. Both my brother and I had used bicycles. His was purchased for $5.00 from strangers. As they became scarcer, mine cost $45.00 from a church family. We also had winter sleds, ice skates, and a big back yard for croquet. My brother had a beautiful electric train, and I had my dollhouse. Those were lean years, but good years — years to build and plan and dream.

If we didn't have much, I wasn't aware of any lack. In our neighborhood almost everyone was in the same situation. Few mothers worked outside of the home; most families had single incomes. We always had plenty to eat and clean, appropriate clothes. We always had a little money saved, too, even though my illnesses depleted the savings regularly. Dad had once been hospitalized for surgery, too, and Mother had fallen down our stairs and split her knee open. My brother seemed to be the strongest, healthiest family member. His childhood illnesses were not severe, and his only hospitalization was for a tonsilectomy.

I thought of us as a "typical" family. We were taught respect and old-fashioned values. We were expected to work hard and to do our best. For my brother and me that meant following the examples of our parents. I never thought of our lives as a tumult on a wild, restless sea. But then I did not know just how severely our Christian family was going to be tested.

I Need Thee, Oh, I Need Thee

I knew I wasn't well that Wednesday morning when I returned to work, but I wasn't really sick either. I had stayed home from work on Monday and spent most of the day in bed, drawing and reading. I watched the workmen around the house finish putting a new coat of stucco on the exterior. Tuesday I had been a bit more active, so on Wednesday I pleaded to go to work. The fever and chills had disappeared, and I thought I was needed at the library. Reluctantly, Mother let me go with my promise to come home if I felt worse.

Our family rarely gave in to sickness. We always tried to carry on and do what others expected of us. I guess that is what I tried to do that morning. The air in the upstairs reference department had a still, heavy quality—as if it had been baking there too long. The door to the attic had been open for weeks in the hope that some cool breeze would stray through the roof ventilators from the outside. Usually all that came in was a confused pigeon or two that had to be caught by the janitor at night. It was hot—stifling hot—but most people worked in hot places in those days.

The heat kept many patrons away, so the library was quiet. When this occurred, I had a continuing task to keep me busy. In 1935 Elgin had celebrated its centennial, and a special commemorative edition had been published by the local newspaper. For some reason, the stories from that edition had never been clipped and filed for reference purposes. Stories were marked in red, and I had inherited the task of cutting them apart, following them through their continuation pages, and marking them for filing. I gathered my newspapers and scissors and headed for a table to work. I welcomed the chance for a sit-down job as I was feeling weak.

21

I worked away only half concentrating. Who needed these clippings anyway? If no one had needed them in fourteen years, was it likely someone would now? I was probably feeling just a little bit sorry for myself. I thought I needed a cooler place to work or a nice iced coke or maybe a chance to lie down for awhile. Actually, I needed so much more.

> *I need Thee, Oh, I need Thee!*
> *Ev'ry hour I need Thee!*
> *Oh, bless me now, my Savior;*
> *I come to Thee!*

Sometime in the early afternoon I was aware of a blinding, stabbing pain in my head. I closed my eyes and rested briefly, but the pain would neither leave nor lessen. I tried to focus my eyes on the newsprint, but the columns blurred. I felt slightly nauseous. My sight had snapped into a blurred confusion.

I sat at the table wondering what I should do. I knew I had to get home, but there was no way I could walk the 12 blocks. I couldn't read my watch to see what time the next bus would be. I was sure I did not have enough money with me to pay for a taxi. We seldom used cabs in our family, and I was unaware that I could have called a cab and paid for it when I arrived home.

Slowly I folded the newspapers and gathered the clipped stories, scissors, and scraps. I tried to get up, but the room spun. I couldn't get the walls and furniture in focus. Carefully I walked to the desk and reported, "I have to go home. I'm sick."

"Do you want to call home?" the librarian asked.

"Yes." I intended to call my mother and have her get my uncle to come for me. He had the kind of business that he could leave anytime, and I felt this was an emergency. When I tried the phone, the line was busy. I tried again, but it was still busy.

I must have looked very ill, for the librarian took over calling for me. Since we had a party line, the librarian asked the operator to cut in on the call to try to free the line. The caller was not my mother, and the other lady said her call was not completed yet. She would not give up the line. I didn't know what else to do.

I felt as if my legs could not support me, and the dizziness from my blurred vision and the throbbing in my head were making me increasingly nauseous. I knew I *had* to get home. In my weakness and confusion I couldn't think. Some instinct told me with each throb in my head: get home, get home, get home. Dear God, get me home, I prayed.

I turned away from the desk to go to the bus stop a block and a half away, and no one stopped me. Fortunately, I knew the library steps by heart and could get down them with my eyes shut, which is what I had to do. Outside I stumbled to the corner and crossed the street. Then I walked beside the building holding to the walls to keep from falling. I do not believe any of the adults who worked at the library had a car that day and could have given me a ride home. Apparently no one thought to loan me taxi money. Maybe I had put on too good an act that morning.

I stood in the August sun leaning against the police station and waited for my bus. A neighbor girl appeared and wanted to talk. I was relieved to have her there because I knew I couldn't read the street names on the buses, but I could board whichever one she did.

"Are you all right?" she asked.

"I'm so sick, Barb," I told her.

"What's wrong?"

"I don't know," I told her honestly, and I almost cried. When our bus came, she wanted to sit with me on the ride home. "No, I'm too sick." Although I know now that it was the double vision that kept me from walking properly, the weakness and my unsure gait made me think I might have polio. I did not want to expose anyone, so I rode alone in the back of the bus. My stop was before Barb's, and I got off with a retired policeman who lived across the street. He would later relate that I was so unsteady he thought he would have to carry me home. I stumbled alone though.

As I walked the block home, I became aware that our car was in the driveway. My father and brother were home. Had I been able to reach Mother by phone, she would have sent my own father to pick me up. The injustice of my difficult trip home and the frustration of my weakness overwhelmed me. I began to cry, but I was home. God had gotten me home.

Somehow I moved upstairs and into bed; maybe my father carried me. Mother called the doctor who promised to come around the supper hour. The intense throbbing in my head increased so that I felt the vibrations of the floor if someone walked in my room. Mother tiptoed in and out, eager to get something or do something for me, but I was beyond her help at that particular time.

Later I heard my brother climb the stairs and stop at the door to my room. "Don't come in," I pleaded.

"I just brought your jacket upstairs," he said.

"Hang it on the doorknob," I told him, "Don't come in. I don't want you to get whatever I've got." He quietly walked away, frustrated by the same helplessness stunning my parents.

The doctor came in the twilight hours. He was puzzled and hazarded a diagnosis of encephalitis—a brain fever. He knew I should be hospitalized at once. Arrangements were made for an ambulance to transport me. Somewhere in my subconscious I was relieved that he had not said polio.

When the ambulance men were stymied by the curve of the stairway, I offered to try to walk to the stretcher, but Mother insisted they come to the bedroom and carry me. I think I may have passed out briefly after I was placed on the stretcher because I recall nothing of the inevitable jostling that must have occurred on the trip down the stairs and out to the ambulance.

Mother rode with me in the ambulance, and Dad followed in the car. I remember going north on Spring Street with the last rays of daylight filtering through the giant trees arched above us. Mother sat grimly beside me, steeling herself with prayer and determination for whatever would come next. I searched for something to lighten her anguish and made a feeble attempt at humor. "Well, at least we'll be arriving in style," I told her.

She was too distraught to pretend the situation was anything other than what it was. "This is nothing to joke about," she snapped curtly. "You'd better be saying your prayers."

I didn't care enough to try to talk anymore. I may have been given a sedative to endure the ambulance trip, or maybe the fever was again blurring my thinking. Exactly what happened was lost to me.

We became separated. Parents were probably not allowed in the isolation ward. I was in a room by myself, being helped into a hospital gown by a kindly nurse's aide. I couldn't see well enough to get acquainted with my new surroundings. I climbed gingerly into bed, and she smoothed the sheets around me. I knew my manners and tried to answer her small talk politely, but I felt so weak.

The last thing I remember about that night was trying to focus on her as she stood by the door.

"Is there anything I can get you before I go?" she asked.

"No, thank you," I whispered. The fierce pounding in my head was intensifying, obliterating my efforts to be alert and cooperative.

"If you need anything overnight, just put your light on," she said as she gently closed the door.

Need anything?

I need Thee, Oh, I need Thee!

While I Draw
This Fleeting Breath

Hospitals were not frightening to me; I had been in them too often. Yet this time something was definitely different; something was very wrong. Whenever it was that I awoke the next morning or became conscious that it was day, I knew I was not well. Someone brought in my breakfast tray and cranked up my bed. On the tray was a copy of the morning *Tribune*, compliments of a local dairy. I could figure out none of the dizzying print except the giant headline, but I thought it would be nice to save the paper for Mother (we did not subscribe at home) assuming she would be coming to see me later.

I remember clearly that there was a dish of apricots on the tray. Although not really hungry, I intended to be the good patient and eat my food. However, I couldn't get the fruit on my spoon. I took my fork and attempted to stab the elusive halves, but my fork never struck where the fruit was. I had no skills to cope with this visual impairment, so I left the food where it was and ate the toast. I didn't want to feel for canned fruit with my fingers and pick it up in my hands to eat by instinct. When the nurse returned for the tray, I explained my problem. She made a notation that I would need to be fed—one extra responsibility in an already overworked ward.

I was admitted to what had been children's court but was then converted to the isolation ward to accommodate the large number of polio cases in that prevaccine summer. I was told that whatever personal belongings I brought into the ward would eventually be destroyed. Family members allowed to visit critical cases all had to be masked and gowned. Some visiting was done through the windows to friends and relatives on the driveway and sidewalks one floor below. I can recall no visitors, but I remember hearing the calls of others outside the windows. Many of the nurses and aides were in the ward because they volunteered. Many others refused the duty because of the hazard involved; no one knew how the contagious disease was spread. I learned later that some doctors with young children in their families checked on their patients by consulting with the nurses at the door to the ward. Our beloved Dr. Partridge was not one of these, though he had a young family. He came at least once every day during my entire hospitalization.

That first breakfast is one of the last things I remember. During the day I know a nurse held me on my side while a doctor performed a spinal tap to determine if I had polio. I must have asked about getting our old radio if I would still be in the hospital that following Saturday. Lauritz Melchior was to be the featured artist at the Chicagoland Music Festival, and I wanted to hear him.

Although I remember nothing of any visit, I do remember a nurse bringing a new plastic radio which my dad had bought for me. I know how guilty I felt getting a new radio since I had been told anything with me in the isolation ward would have to be destroyed. I did try to listen to it, though I cannot be sure if I ever heard the music festival or not.

I had been moved or given a roommate, a younger girl, and there was something wrong with her that registered through my own pain and distorted vision. She cried pitifully and looked at me with piercing black eyes, but I could not help her. I think she wanted me to do something with the radio, and I recall turning the dial for her and wondering at the stiffness in my once-agile fingers. I remember nothing more for a long time.

Whatever happened for the next few weeks is blessedly blotted out of my mind. I know that I developed the respiratory problems common to so many polio victims. At some time I was put in an oxygen tent to help me breathe. My mother was told that there was no hope—a message she had been given once before many years earlier after my ruptured appendix. She was told to prepare me to die. I must have drifted in and out of consciousness, for she tells how she tried to reassure me that I had nothing to fear, that I had been a good girl and would go to heaven to be with Jesus. I am told that I replied that I didn't want to go to heaven—that I didn't know anybody there.

My breathing apparently grew more ragged as the fever raged throughout my body.

> *While I draw this fleeting breath,*
> *When mine eyelids close in death,*
> *When I soar to worlds unknown . . .*
> *. . . . .*
> *Thou must save, and Thou alone.*

My doctor was not in the ward when I reached a critical low, and another physician stepped in and made the decision to put me in an iron lung. Freed from the labor of breathing, my body endured the relentless fever. Some days later the balance tipped in favor of life, and I survived. I have to believe that God wanted me to live, for much of my world had collapsed around me.

The first stimulus to register on my brain was the fluorescent glow that I became aware of out in the hall. A blue neon QUIET sign hung above the doors at the far end of the ward. That light attracted my subconscious mind, dragging me back to the world of the living and harsh reality.

Help of
the Helpless

I awoke to a world I did not want. Everything but my head was encased in a huge metal canister that did my breathing for me. I could no longer breathe by myself. That was only the first of the countless could-nots that had taken over my life. Of course, I could not see properly. I could not move any parts of my body. I could not feed myself and could not swallow well when food was placed in my mouth. I could not walk, could not sit up, and could not even turn over on the narrow cot within the iron lung. I could not talk in complete sentences unless they were short ones because I had to stop exhaling when the machine did and breathe in with it — mid-sentence or not. I could not sit up, since iron lungs do not bend, and neither could I anymore. Worst of all for those around me, I could not adjust.

I shared a room with another iron lung victim — a sparkling, six-year-old girl named Darlene. The ward adored her; probably the whole hospital did. She had beautiful, long, dark hair. The nurses often tied a bow in it as it hung down in shining curls from the headrest of her lung. Her snapping, dark eyes looked into the mirror above her, following the activities of the ward. Her smile was irresistible and her laughter frequent.

In contrast, I had bald patches on my head where the high fever had caused my hair to fall out. My eyes could not focus on the mirror or turn from their fixed positions. I could turn my head only slightly, not enough to see even if I had been able to focus. My face was twisted grotesquely by the paralysis that had claimed my body. I was grouchy and difficult. I felt nobody loved me. Even the minister eventually found it necessary to scold me for my attitude.

28

I was stunned and confused by what had happened to my strong, once-responsive body. Not too patiently, I was waiting to get well, but nothing was happening. A therapist came and reached in through the portholes on my lung to check my range of motion. There was almost none. Only my right arm could be persuaded to draw up across my chest when it was straightened. Sometimes the drag against the cotton sheets was too much to overcome, and I could not move it at all. The fingers of my left hand curled feebly when held away from my body. Nothing else moved. I was cross and irritable and cried often. I was sick of being told to try to move legs that no longer moved, to wiggle toes that no longer wiggled, to lift hands that no longer responded—to try, try, try. How could I transmit messages over a nervous system so massively destroyed? Why was God letting this happen to me?

Another battle paralleled the attack on motion. Often my iron lung would be unplugged to see if I could breathe again. I would use my last gasp of air to cry out that I couldn't breathe, and the machine would be started again. Darlene was ahead of me in the recovery process, breathing a few minutes at a time on her own. Our lungs would be stopped at the same time, but hers could stay off much longer than mine. She was even better than I was at breathing. For me panic set in after 10 seconds of independent breathing. I needed that respirator! Gradually, I began to breathe on my own again, using stomach muscles instead of the paralyzed chest muscles—30 seconds at a time, several times a day. The weakened diaphragm responded slowly—60 seconds. The coaxing and pleading for me to try continued—two minutes.

Although I was unaware of it, my iron lung was unique. Stored away was a hood that could be attached over the headrest portion and could maintain the breathing function while the lung itself was opened at the regular place. This would allow the patient to be exposed for medical care without interrupting the breathing support and without forcing the doctors to work through the limiting porthole openings on each side, which allowed only the forearms to be inserted through the tight cuffs. Thus, for example, an emergency appendectomy could be performed on a patient in a lung.

I didn't need this feature, but it was the nearest lung available when my crisis approached. Lungs were hauled all over from hospital to hospital wherever a need arose. Somewhere a pregnant young woman needed my lung so she could give birth to her child while she was in a respirator. I was to be transferred to another lung that had hastily been brought in.

I was told what was going to be done and why, and I panicked. I was safe and secure inside my metal canister; I didn't want to move. They could get her a lung somewhere else. Why couldn't they have needed Darlene's lung; she could breathe longer. They could never transfer me out of one lung into another in less than two minutes; I would die! I wanted to help the stricken young woman in some way, but not this way. It wasn't fair!

Fortunately, I didn't have a choice. The second lung was opened just outside my room, plugged in and ready. My lung was opened. Strong arms slid under me, gently pulling my head back through its snug rubber cuff. I was lifted and swiftly carried horizontally the few steps to the cot of the second lung. I was quickly positioned; the cot was slid back inside; the lung was closed; and breathing was restored — well under two minutes! Afterwards, they said I had been brave, but I was not brave. I was a coward without a choice.

Enough time passed that the ward was no longer dealing with a local epidemic. The case load leveled off. Eventually, my parents could come for their visits without donning the once mandatory gowns over their regular clothing. I recognized them by their voices. With my poor vision and from my prone position in the respirator, I saw them only as fuzzy outlines against the white ceiling. How eagerly they awaited each day's bulletin that I had breathed on my own for 60 seconds or two minutes. Three minutes seemed to be my maximum, a long plateau that I couldn't seem to pass.

I often asked about my brother. He had written to me when I was first hospitalized because he was not allowed in the isolation ward, but I had heard no more from him. I was reassured that he was just too busy adjusting to college to write. After all, school had started. My friends were in classes, but not I. I had always loved school and done well without much effort, yet deep within me was a gnawing concern that I would be falling far behind my classmates if I had to stay in the hospital much longer. I found relief in knowing that my medical bills were being taken care of, for I would have been in anguish if I had thought my parents were using my brother's college funds for my lengthy hospitalization.

Friends tried to cheer me with lots of get-well cards. Mother or the nurses read them to me, as I could neither see nor hold them. I thought of the red corduroy suit I was planning to wear to school that fall. Would I be well in time? Not likely if I couldn't even get out of the iron lung!

Day after day the lung would be opened while a nurse watched me breathe and timed me. When I would plead to have the lung closed again and the pressure restored, I was told that if I still had the breath to beg, I didn't need to go back in yet. That was logical, but the frightening alternative seemed to be that I couldn't go back in until I stopped breathing.

While other patients practiced walking, my recovery was measured in seconds and minutes of independent breathing. I was the worst polio case. Even Darlene and I breathed to different drums.

Darlene could have her iron lung opened and breathe on her own for nearly a half hour at a time. Miss West would read to her to keep her mind occupied, but Miss West *knew* that I wasn't trying or I could do it too.

"Do you want to listen?" she would ask.

"Yes."

"Then you'll have to leave the lung open, too."

"No," I would protest. "I can't breathe."

"Then you can't listen," she would counter.

"But I can't," I would wheedle; "please!"

But there was no babying and no compromise in Miss West's system. She would push my lung as far away as possible to keep me from hearing the story. Then she would sit with her back toward me right beside Darlene's headrest and read very softly. She thought that I would not be able to hear above the heavy wheezing of the respirator and that would punish me for not trying.

Miss West did not realize how keen my hearing had become in the absence of good vision. I could identify most of the nurses walking in the hall outside my room by their footsteps. I knew all the regular people by their voices. I could hear the story, though not easily, and I followed the adventures of the little colt Misty just as Darlene did. Tears of frustration welled in my eyes. Crying was not easy in an iron lung that permitted no gasp of a sob nor any way to wipe a tear—even if I could have moved. Besides, I did not want Miss West to know how badly I felt.

I think I hated Miss West. I know that when she fed me, I ate less. My poor eating concerned everyone. The flesh seemed to waste away from day to day, and no food tempted my appetite. Miss Huber, who said I could call her Lois, joshed and teased me into eating a few bites. That was not Miss West's way. She would dump the first spoonful of food into my mouth and be poised above my face with the second before I had even swallowed.

"Open up," she would command. "Nobody eats that slow."

I do, I thought. I would open my mouth a slit to try to prevent her from putting the whole serving in at once.

"I don't have all day," she would complain as she forced my teeth apart with the spoon. "There are other patients here besides you, you know."

"I'm through," I would announce clamping my mouth shut.

"Do you want me to hold your nose shut?" This persuasion hardly elicited my cooperation.

"I'm full," I would say, "I can't eat any more." I knew Mother would be disappointed to hear I had only eaten two spoonfuls for lunch. I just never felt like eating when Miss West fed me.

I know I was often unpleasant. I know my disposition matched my ugly, twisted face. No one, least of all I, seemed to recognize what a traumatic adjustment I was trying to cope with. Yet only Miss West complained about the poor grace with which I was accepting my new life. She regularly told the minister about my shortcomings, usually within my hearing. He felt compelled to chide me about my attitude and my Christian example. Yet I seemed as powerless to change my personality as I was to move my body.

Pastor Schuth did not give up on me though. As faithfully as my doctor came to see me, Pastor Schuth came, too. He also was a young man who had small children at home, but he didn't avoid the exposure to polio either. He sat beside my iron lung talking and praying, and often he sang. He encouraged me to sing again—even in that respirator. He sang with me, pacing the words and phrases of familiar hymns to the rhythmic breathing in and out of the lung. What a strange duet that must have been drifting out the door and through the corridor of the ward.

> *Abide with me! Fast falls the eventide;*
> *The darkness deepens; Lord, with me abide.*
> *When other helpers fail and comforts flee,*
> *Help of the helpless, oh, abide with me!*

The pastor's strong tenor must have sustained my shaky soprano as he labored to put a song back in my heart. I sang the words, but I was unaware of the break my heart was yet to suffer or of how deep the darkness would become. I was still much too sick to comprehend everything that had happened to me. I did not recognize how totally helpless I had become, nor did I suspect how permanent my condition could be. There was no other option except to abide in the Lord and trust in Him.

Be Still, My Soul

After some time I began to breathe for longer periods with the lung opened. Ten minutes became 15; 30 minutes became an hour; an hour became two or three. When the independent breathing was long enough to warrant the effort, I was removed from the lung and placed on a hospital bed. Two or three nurses working together would slide me down on the lung's cot so that my head came through the rubber collar and then place their arms under me and carry me in a horizontal position. My weight was down to less than 70 pounds, but my five-foot-seven-inch height made me awkward to move without bending.

Sometimes I could stay out a half a day, but I worried about breathing alone. The exertion of pumping air in and out was tiring. It was always a relief to be returned to the lung and have the steady machine take over. I spent nights in the lung because I was afraid that when I fell asleep, I would forget to breathe. When that final barrier was overcome and I could exist for 24 hours without needing the lung, I was moved to a regular room. It was a lovely corner room with treetops visible outside both windows. The leaves were already tinged with gold. I was ready for the next stage of recovery.

One morning there was something different about the routine. I was bathed and fed early. Several nurses peeked in the door to see that I was ready. I was alone in my room when Dr. Partridge came in and stood beside my bed. He held my hand as he talked about my brother. I began to understand that my brother too had polio, but my mind could not quite grasp the implications. I usually had my illnesses alone while the entire family waited on me. Now were there two of us ill with polio? Did the doctor mean that Sonny was here in the hospital in some other room?

"He was here," he told me, but I didn't recognize the

33

significance of the past tense.

"Then where is he now?" I had been told he was already at college, too busy to write.

The words tortured the doctor. "Mary, we lost Bud."

Even now as I write these words, I can recall the wrenching grief. I could not even wipe my eyes that streamed with tears. My mind rebelled. Not Sonny! He was so strong he could pick up all 120 pounds of me and carry me upstairs. He was six feet, two inches tall and had seldom been sick in his life. He was so good, so kind, so honest, so gentle, so hard-working, so patient, so intelligent, so much better than I. He could not die—not at age 17!

Pastor Schuth was waiting in the hall, and he came in to explain to me what had happened—not that I could understand. They had waited to tell me until I was strong enough to hear the news. I learned later that they had delayed my brother's funeral a day, expecting me to die, so that we could be buried together. All those days and weeks when I had asked about him, they had gently lied to me, telling me that he was busy at college when he was actually dead. I had never suspected the awful truth.

When the doctor and the minister left, some of the nurses came in. Everyone had known except me. How could I have been so blind? They explained that at first I had been so ill that I was not conscious of anything. Afterwards when my mind was alert again, only the staff, Pastor Schuth, and my parents saw me. My mail was read to me since I could neither see nor hold it. If someone would have written about Sonny, that part would never have been read to me.

My mind could not take it in. "But where was he? What room was he in?"

"He was across the hall," Lois explained gently.

"But why didn't anybody tell me?" They had let me believe everything was all right and let me ask my stupid questions.

"You were too sick to know." It had been a conspiracy of compassion.

Finally, I was left alone in my misery. It would be almost three hours before Mother came for her daily visit. She would be told that I now knew. My grief swirled around me. I felt as if all my insides had been torn out leaving only an empty shell that looked like me.

Oh, Sonny, Sonny! How could I ever make it up to him for all the trouble I'd caused him? How many times I had teased him until he finally retaliated and tickled me or held my arms pinned to my side so I couldn't punch him. As soon as he would try to defend himself, I would scream for my mother's attention. Sometimes we would both be scolded, but he was always lectured because he "was older and should know better." Oh, why had I done that?

Oh, Sonny, I'm so sorry! I remembered the times I had ordered him out of my room as if it were private property. Yet how often I

34

had played in his room. I used his globe and books to play school. I played with his train when I was so little he worried I'd break it. I listened to the radio on his bed and painted. Was I ever anything to him but a nuisance?

I thought of all the people who must be missing him terribly— his friends Donn and Hugh, little Carol next door who loved him so, and too many people to even count. What would we all do now? How could we live without him?

My mind could not yet thank God for the time we had him. I could not yet absorb the tragedy. I must have been well enough to know the truth because I suffered no relapse. The iron lung waiting in the hall was not needed.

In bits and pieces I learned of Sonny's brief illness and sudden death. The doctor had monitored him closely and ordered him to the hospital. My parents were sent home and told to get some rest. Almost immediately they were summoned back and then told to sit and wait. Not being rushed into a sick room alerted them that their child was dead, but they were unprepared when told it was their strong, healthy son who had died of bulbar polio as the doctor worked over him. He had been in his own bed at home just hours before.

As I lay unconscious in an iron lung, my brother lay in his coffin. The news devastated our family and friends, especially in our little church. My uncle was an undertaker, but he could not take care of my brother. My parents made the arrangements with a local mortuary and went through the rites and formalities of death. There was a terrible fear of polio in the community. There had been more than 40 cases and several deaths, includng another teenager who had worked with my brother. My parents were advised to spend $300 for a glass cover for the coffin so that no visitor would feel the danger of contagion, although there actually was no danger.

Regardless of the fears, many people visited the chapel. Many others sent cards. At home more food came than my poor parents could possibly eat. A lunch was arranged in the church basement after the funeral so that no one need fear entering our house. For some this was a very real fear. One man confessed later that he hadn't wanted to be a pallbearer but hadn't known how to refuse my parents when they asked. Even an aunt came over briefly with tissue around her hand so she wouldn't have to touch the doorknob. For some time later, people would visit on the screened porch, but not inside the house.

To the stillness of my body was added another stillness in my soul. My old way of life was completely gone whether I realized it or not. Ahead were only small hopes for any significant recovery. I had always loved the verse, "Be still, and know that I am God" (Ps. 46:10). The God who gave could take away. There was no other consolation.

Be still, my soul;
The Lord is on thy side;
Bear patiently the cross of grief or pain;
Leave to thy God to order and provide;
In every change He faithful will remain.

I Am Weak,
but Thou Art Strong

The golden days of autumn came with the relentlessness of time. The scare of the summer polio epidemic had passed leaving several dead and many wounded. Around me the other victims were practicing walking, strengthening weakened muscles, and exercising tightened ranges of motion. A few were building strong arms and shoulders in preparation for handling the long leg braces they would soon receive. I was the worst casualty, the most seriously afflicted of the survivors.

I was lifted onto a stretcher and wheeled to therapy for the muscle test to assess the damages. The therapist stood beside me, picked up my right hand, and laid the fingers over her left index finger.

"Now squeeze," she said. "Make a fist."

Nothing. She checked each finger individually. Nothing. The first of the columns of zeroes was recorded on the muscle chart.

Delicately she traced her finger along the outside length of my index finger. "Think right here," she said. She feather-touched the skin along my finger again. "Now straighten this finger. Make it point."

Nothing.

Patiently she flexed, extended, turned, bent, and rotated my body at every joint searching for a response. Column after column of zeroes indicated nothing was left. An occasional *T* marked a muscle strand that had shown a trace of motion left, but hardly anything to build with. The therapy would consist of little more than stretching exercises.

The water therapy was equally demoralizing. The buoyancy of

37

water was supposed to reduce the pull of gravity against weakened muscles and allow them to move with less effort. With weakened muscles, yes, but with muscles lost through the destruction of nerve cells, no. My left arm lay just as lifeless in the water as in a bed. My times in the Hubbard tank were spent lying on the inclined stretcher fearing that I would slide downward until my face would slip below the water. My right arm, which had limited motion, had a useless hand. I couldn't even pull myself up if I slipped. I lay as still as possible fearing drowning and defeating the purpose of the treatment.

As much as I liked the therapists, I hated therapy. Everyone else was progressing, lifting weakened arms high in the air, lurching through parallel bars, walking, stretching, and sitting. I was not used to being the poorest in everything, the one who could do the least, the one with the least potential. I was definitely last place!

Along with the daily frustrations of being crippled, I became conscious that summer had flamed into autumn. I had always loved the warmth and haze of fall days, and I longed to be out in them as others were. Since I was unable to bend enough to sit upright at a 90-degree angle, or even a 45-degree position, I was unable to sit in a wheelchair. My weight had dropped by about 60 pounds, and any pressure against my frail body brought pain. It was almost impossible to be comfortable any way except lying flat.

However, Nurse Huber sensed my need to be out of the hospital, even though briefly. She comandeered a stretcher and had me lifted on it. She wrapped me warmly in blankets, maneuvered me outside through the emergency entrance, and took me for "a walk" on a golden day. Except for the fact that lying flat on my back emphasized the severity of the crippling that had occurred, it was a wonderful way to feel the October weather. The trees lining the sidewalk arched over the stretcher with their tracery of branches etched against the sky. Clusters of brilliant, golden leaves clung in random patches here and there. White cloud tufts drifted across the sky. Looking at the sky required no visual focus. I was suddenly reminded of the psalm which begins, "The heavens declare the glory of God; and the firmament showeth his handiwork" (Ps. 19:1). Perhaps that was the day I first realized that God had made autumn especially beautiful to counter man's natural fear of dying. My brother had died; I had not. In my weakness my spirit touched that of the long-ago psalmist when he said, "God is our refuge and strength, a very present help in trouble" (Ps. 46:1). There was a sort of peace that settled on me along with the maple leaves that drifted down onto my stretcher as we headed back. That trip was a brief spiritual renewal before my return to the routine of misery and futile efforts to recover.

Gradually the isolation ward, which had once again become the children's ward, began to lose its polio patients. Many returned to their homes completely well. Their places were taken by regular patients with the usual childhood problems. In a sense we were a family. The consistent dedication of the floor nurses, in an era when nurses provided the actual nursing care, was beautiful. They cared about us.

They taped photos sent by friends to the wall beside my bed. Each day they brushed my heavy hair and tied a ribbon in it to match my nightgown. I had bitten my nails as a nervous, overly energetic child, but they had grown long in the iron lung imprisoned away from my mouth. My piano teacher had sent me a gift of several matching lipsticks and nail polishes, and the nurses polished my nails. They coaxed and teased me to eat and tried so hard to encourage me. I am afraid I repaid them poorly. I know that although I like most of them personally very much, it was difficult for me to adjust to my new condition of dependence.

As the polio patients left, I began to get a succession of roommates. I soon realized that I had become something of a local curiosity, and I dreaded the almost daily change of tonsilectomy roommates. The children and their parents seemed to feel that sharing a room with me made them privy to my case. It was not unusual for roommate's visitors to ask me questions like, "Can you move your legs at all?" or "Can you squeeze your hand like this?" or far more personal questions. Good manners seemed to require that I politely answer adults' questions, but I resented the prying and the constant emphasis on my inabilities.

Fortunately, children were not permitted to visit in the hospital, and visitors were usually limited to parents or close friends in the children's ward. Even so, my mother received calls from people who wanted to know if they could come to see me. Quite literally, this was what they wanted, for they were usually scant acquaintances at best. I did not need to be viewed in my vulnerable weakness, especially since there was nothing any visitor could do that wasn't being done.

Hundreds of people were truly kind. Cards arrived daily. People longed to do something for my parents or me, but there was little to do. So many wanted to send me a get-well present, but what can you send an eighth grader who cannot see to read nor hold a book, cannot handle a jigsaw puzzle or game, is too old for toys and dolls, needs no clothing other than hospital gowns, cannot hold a pen or pencil to write or draw, has no appetite for foods, and has no place for plants or flowers? Many people sent a handkerchief or knick-knack, added a miniature to my dollhouse collection, sent a cup and saucer for the small collection I had started two years earlier with my father's christening cup, bought me a fancy bed jacket or perfume to help me feel more feminine, sent a pretty pin or bracelet, or tempted me with homemade treats. The outpouring of thoughtfulness was overwhelming. It would be impossible to guess how many offered prayers for my recovery and strength for my parents and me to face our uncertain future.

I am weak, but Thou art strong.

Our strength had to come from the Lord. How could Dad be on the job day after day and keep his mind on his work? How could mother meet people every day whose first question was "How's Mary?" How hard for her to have so little to report. Yet there was some progress. I was breathing better. The eye doctor had attempted to correct my double vision with glasses. That had not been successful, but new lenses gave me better vision if I used only one eye at a time. I squinted and tried to see.

My uncle had come with his ambulance and taken me for a ride one day. I had gone home to see the house with its new coat of stucco. Although it did not increase my ability to move, the therapy was reducing my stiffness, and I could bend enough to sit in a reclining wheel-chair for short periods of time.

My voice teacher decided her lessons might help my breathing improve. She obtained permission to use the old upright piano in the nurses' dining room and came to the hospital several times to give me "lessons." These were short because I could not sit for very long. I really could not breathe well enough to sing properly either, but Mrs. Stewart made me think I could sing again.

It became increasingly clear that the local hospital, despite its dedicated staff and good intentions, could not meet the specialized needs of my severe paralysis. Dr. Partridge had made application for me at the Warm Springs Foundation founded by President Roosevelt. This was *the* polio treatment center.

Since I was not told that an application on my behalf had been made, I was not told when it was rejected either. The reason given was that the severity of my case would defeat the purpose of the Warm Springs Foundation. In those heavy plague years the foundation had many more applicants than it could accept. The policy seemed to be to accept those with the greatest potential for recovery. To the aching loss my parents had suffered and the daily frustration of seeing others get well and leave the hospital was added the new heartbreak that their daughter was considered almost beyond hope by the best experts in the field.

Fortunately for me, that first rejection was not taken as final. A reapplication was made. This time a personal letter from the physical therapist at the hospital was also included. She had trained at Warm Springs and knew many of the staff. Prayers were redoubled that the doors might be opened for my admission.

Hopes and Fears
of All the Years

After a death in the family, the first year holds many difficult anniversaries. The first family gatherings, birthdays, and holidays emphasize the loss of the absent member. For us the first Christmas was traumatic. I was young enough to think that Christmas gifts were important, and I wanted gifts for my special nurses and favorite fellow patients. Mother went downtown to shop for the gifts, but she often left the stores without buying anything. The holiday mood in the stores and the Christmas carols playing everywhere saddened her so that she had to go home.

Well-meaning friends tried hard to bring us warmth and show their concerns. Although it must have been difficult to pick appropriate cards for us, we received hundreds of greetings. Local groups caroled through the hospital corridors. The ward nurses planned a Christmas party with several gifts for each patient. Dozens of people shared their Christmas baking with us. Mother kept a list of the avalanche of gifts that poured in for me and eventually wrote thank-you notes for them all.

It was decided that I would go home for Christmas, and my uncle took me home in his ambulance Christmas Eve. There was a tree at home and many, many presents. I had no wheelchair and couldn't sit up long anyway, so I stayed on the wheeled ambulance stretcher. Our dear neighbor Les and Dad carried me upstairs that night to sleep in my own bed. Together they carried me back down the next day, and a steady stream of visitors dropped in all day. I was dressed in the jacket of the red corduroy suit I had bought for school, but it was now paired with red corduroy slacks that hid my pitiful thinness.

Amid all the excitement, my mother prepared the holiday turkey dinner, which was a welcome change from hospital cooking. I felt surrounded by good intentions.

Yet the contrasts with previous Christmases could not be ignored. I lay on my stretcher close to the floor and looked up as my aunt at the piano played the carols I had played the year before. I could not even reach up to touch the keyboard. Our traditional holiday menu was the same, but I was fed my dinner. The guests included relatives plus my nurse Lois and her widowed mother. Schoolmates delivered the present that they had collected money to buy for me, and I could sense how terribly uncomfortable my illness made them. A neighbor brought a gift and turned away in tears when she realized I could not take the package she held out toward my crippled hands. Through all the forced festivities was an aching emptiness.

I felt a certain relief to be back in the ambulance, silently gliding up snow-packed Spring Street back to the hospital. My world was no longer the world of active, able people; my world was the sheltered security of the hospital where many are frail and helpless.

That first Christmas without Sonny held a special anguish. Pastor Schuth addressed that grief when he gave us a card bearing the following poem written by his friend Alice Hansche Mortenson:

For You Who Mourn at Christmas Time

For you who mourn at Christmas time,
I breathe a special prayer
That God may grant you inner peace
And strength your cross to bear.

That you may look beyond your tears,
Beyond the vacant chair,
And lean your heavy heart on Him
Who waits your grief to share.

That through your loss you may, somehow,
This year have more to give
To this dark world because of Him
Who died that we might live.

That you may rise above your grief
To clasp another's hand
In loving, gentle sympathy,
Because you understand.

That even now you'll hear the song
Of "Peace, Good Will to Men,"
And never lose the blessed road
That leads to Bethlehem.

And so for you at Christmas time
I breathe a special prayer
That in the dark you'll always see
His star is shining there.

How true that the star shining over Bethlehem was still shining over our world. For us the season was etched with hope — the certain hope that our family would someday be reunited, the hope that our destiny was guided by One far wiser than we, the hope of the coming new year and the new decade, and the hope of healing at the Georgia Warm Springs Foundation where I had finally been accepted.

A beloved carol haunted my mind that Christmas night.

Yet in thy darkness shineth
The everlasting Light;
The hopes and fears Of all the years
Are met in thee tonight.

A Balm in Gilead

The elaborate plans for my transfer to the polio center in Warm Springs, Georgia, were all made. Since I could sit up (in a reclining position) for less than an hour, both air and car travel were impossible. I was to go in a train compartment accompanied by my nurse Lois Huber. My uncle would transport me by ambulance to the Chicago station. The Chicago and Eastern Railroad was prepard to remove a window to get me on board if Dad and Uncle Clyde could not carry me in a horizontal position around the narrow corridor turns. At the Atlanta station an ambulance from the foundation would meet me with drivers who were used to getting patients on and off and in and out of all kinds of conveyances.

Dad and Mother would drive down in our car loaded with light housekeeping needs, as Mother would be renting a furnished apartment in the village of Warm Springs to be near me. The wife and little daughter of another patient from our area would share the apartment with her, since housing was scarce in the area. This arrangement would cut expenses for both.

We left Illinois in mid-January. Dad and Uncle Clyde were able to get me on board without train alterations. It was the first time I would be traveling without family, and my helpessness made me somewhat apprehensive. However, the trip went smoothly. The only problem was that the train stopped several times during the night. Lois would look out to see if we were at a station, but we never were. We were passing through areas suffering heavy winter flooding that occasionally forced the train to stop. We arrived eight hours late in Atlanta.

I arrived at the Warm Springs Foundation shortly after the supper hour on a cold, damp night. I was somewhat sick from the strain and exhausted, but a temporary bed and supper were ready for me. Knowing, capable hands assumed my care, and soft, accented voices welcomed me. By the time my parents arrived a day later, I was rested and settled in my own room.

Patients at the foundation led a far more vigorous life than hospital patients. For one thing, they were given daily tub baths. For another, they were dressed every day in street clothes complete with shoes. There was a full social life as well as medical treatments. Many patients ate together in the dining hall. It seemed far different from hospital life.

After my initial tests and examinations, I was assigned a wheelchair and allowed to sit up. Because of the slight spinal curvature I had already developed, I was fitted for a corset. Nearly everyone wore one for better support in sitting. It was sewn of stiff canvas-like material reinforced with metal stays. Every effort was made to make the garment comfortable, but it always seemed to rub or chafe somewhere. Within 10 days of my arrival I had my first hand splints, and my personal wheelchair was fitted with arm slings. These supported my weakened shoulders.

The attitude of the patients was warm and friendly. Our common bond of polio united us, and friendships came easily. They came from all parts of the country, and few had a family member with them as I had Mother. Although at first I was in a private room, I quickly met many patients. One evening just after supper I was lying on my bed when I heard a lovely soprano voice drifting across the hall. It seemed to be coming from Susan's room. Since I knew the song, I joined in softly.

The song changed to one I had learned in the young people's group at church. "Oh, tell me why the stars do shine."

This time I joined in as strongly as I could. "Oh, tell me why the ivy twines."

Susan must have heard me, for when I began the third line, "Oh, tell me why the sky's so blue," she was singing a clear, beautiful harmony above me.

As we finished the second verse, an attendant came into my room. "Y'all givin' us a free concert?" she asked.

"Are we disturbing somebody?" I asked.

"Heavens no!" she assured me. "It's better'n a radio. Y'all keep goin'."

Mother came back from her supper in the dining hall, opened the back door to East Wing, and heard us singing. She thought it was better than a radio, too.

Susan and I sang together several evenings while we were in those rooms. She had replaced Pastor Schuth as my singing partner. We found that we knew many songs, and she knew descant or alto parts to most. We both sang best lying flat, so we never sang together from one room. Many people heard us, and one man thought we should try to perform together — on records or radio. He offered to

45

make inquiries for us, but we both had other priorities at the moment.

One of those priorities was physical therapy twice a day. Miss Wilson was assigned to be my therapist. Usually in the morning I had table exercises stretching tightened muscles to increase my range of motion. In the afternoon I was usually lifted to the floor by a pushboy to work on a mat where Miss Wilson tried to encourage any wiggle or squirm that might lead to an eventual movement, even hitching a shoulder or arching my back.

By the end of January I had my first pool treatment in the fabled warm waters. The water actually had no therapeutic benefit other than its natural warmness, but the buoyancy lessened gravity's force against weakened muscles. Patients and therapists were in bathing suits. I was lowered into the pool by a strong pushboy. Miss Wilson was waiting to receive me across her arms. She floated me over to one of a dozen treatment tables fastened to the pool floor. Ambulatory patients walked around the edges; others swam or sat in the chairs doing independent exercises. I was less afraid of drowning as Miss Wilson stayed with me always, but the water did not help me much. Very few of those muscle traces were strengthening.

It became quite evident again that, even among hundreds of polio victims, I was very nearly the most severely involved. Certainly I would have been on everyone's list of the worst 10. No one else had the eye paralysis. Few others had lost a family member to polio. "Oh, tell me why."

Although the medical staff did not expect me to get much better, they knew ways they could help me. The first was to teach me to feed myself again. Since my right hand was useless, it was impossible for me to hold a fork or spoon. This challenge had been met before by the creative bracemakers. I experimented with a series of adapted utensils. The best type proved to be those fitted with rings that slipped over my fingers. A fork and spoon were made for me personally. Once it was secured to my hand, I could raise the fork to my mouth with my limited arm and shoulder muscles. I did a poor job of feeding myself in bed, but in my wheelchair with a lap board and the arm slings I could do much better. Unfortunately, my appetite did not return with my feeding proficiency. My comb, lipstick, and toothbrush were also fitted with special attachments so I could use them myself. Since it was obvious I would need a wheelchair of my own, a portable metal chair was ordered to fit my requirements.

In the middle of February I was moved to a four-bed ward with three roommates my age. By then I sat up three times a day and fed myself at least one meal in one of those hour-long sitting sessions. One of the aides gave me my first haircut since polio and trimmed my front hair into bangs. I began to feel less like a patient and more like a person.

My favorite treatments were in occupational therapy. I was learning to use my hand splints and gain control of the erratic muscles that still functioned in my right arm so that I might write again. In late March I drew a dog's head with a crayon and knew for certain that any future career in design was out of the question. I did not have enough pressure to bear down on either crayon or pencil, but some painting was possible. Lacking good control, I used stencils to help me paint the paper or fabric where I wanted to.

In therapy I saw and used my first electric typewriter — a wonderful IBM. However, it had two serious drawbacks for me. If I just glancingly touched the wrong key, the letter was instantly typed on my paper. And if I failed to release the gentlest touch from a key quickly enough, the key kept repeating until I had a string of several extra letters in a word. Since I was typing with the motion of my right arm and using a pencil fastened upside down to my hand splint, accuracy was not my strong point. My first attempt was a few lines of greetings to my father that I called a letter.

Life was much fuller. On my very first Sunday at the foundation, I was surprised to be invited to attend church even though I was not yet allowed to sit up. I accepted and joined several others who were pushed on stretchers to a nondenominational chapel right on the grounds across the road from the main dining hall. It was built in the shape of a cross. Pews occupied a small space for staff and visitors. Most of the floor space was open for wheelchairs and stretchers. More than half of the choir members were in wheelchairs also. I was recruited to sing in the choir before I could sit up (probably on the basis of my evening concerts with Susan), and I attended my first practices on a stretcher. Every Sunday evening there was a fellowship hour in the main lobby of Georgia Hall.

School-aged patients were enrolled in the school program for a five-dollar-a-week additional charge. The more active were full-time students keeping up with their classmates at home. I too resumed studies but on a far more limited basis. I was tutored daily in my room in the ward.

First-run movies were shown three times a week in an old converted stable. Since the danger of fire was always present in the old wooden structure, no movie was ever shown without having the fire truck parked outside with hoses connected and ready. This was a necessary precaution with so many patrons on stretchers and in wheelchairs. Because we had seldom attended movies when I was a child, getting to see all those free movies was a treat. Before I could sit up long enough, I attended on a stretcher with an inclined back rest. I turned my head to see the screen.

There were other special treats for patients. On Franklin Roosevelt's birthday all of us returned from therapy to find gift boxes of candy on our beds. Once a manufacturer sent hundreds of new boys' shirts, and every patient picked one free. Mail from home provided much moral support. Twice my aunt sent packages containing new clothes—pedal pushers, a sweater, a shirt, or a blouse. A few others sent candy, books, jewelry, and other reminders that we were not forgotten.

One day an aide entered my room singing, "Happy birthday to you." She was delivering mail and stopped at my bed with a giant handful. "Happy birthday, dear Mary, happy birthday to you," she finished with a flourish and handed the mail to Mother.

"But it's not my birthday," I told her.

"Aw, you can't fool me. Is your birthday tomorrow?" she wondered.

"It's not even this month," Mother told her and began opening the first of more than 30 cards. We were more mystified than the aide. There were no birthday cards among them, but all wished me well. Not one was signed with a name we recognized.

The next day the aide appeared with over 40 cards. "Somethin' funny is goin' on here," she declared.

Again we recognized no sender, but there was an explanation. One envelope contained a letter explaining that my name had been submitted and was read over a Chicago radio station naming me shut-in-of-the-week. For over a week I received extra mail. All of those people who did not know me were responding to their Christian commitment to do unto one of the least of these. I was astonished and humbled that so many had copied down my name and sent cards—well over a hundred in all plus many letters. Several expressed a desire to correspond with me, but the scanty lines typed to my father represented the whole of my output. Instead, Mother acknowledged our appreciation to the radio station with a letter that was read over the air.

Mother came to see me every day, usually arriving in early afternoon and staying until after the evening meal. She would walk over enjoying the mild winter and take the taxi home at night. She did many services for me and for my roommates who had no relatives nearby. There wasn't too much work in the little apartment she shared, and she needed to escape for her own sanity. There was always something to do at the foundation and a good meal to buy.

A good friend of Mother's visited us and recognized that I shouldn't be the only one receiving special attention. She insisted Mother go with her to Manchester for a shopping trip and buy herself a new dress. Mother needed the change and agreed. Several dresses looked good on Mother, and she selected one. As she was coming out of the fitting room, the clerk was putting two dresses into a bag.

"Oh, no," Mother said, "I'm only buying the striped one."

"Your friend has already paid for the other one for you," the clerk said. Many people were kind. Our beloved Pastor Schuth, no longer able to visit in person, sent letters of care and concern. Visitors were always a special treat. Several visitors stopped in, especially our northern friends on their way to or from Florida vacations. My room-mates' visitors became mine, too.

The days quickly filled and passed. Although I was doing more things, I was not truly getting better. I still had the same useless limbs and the limited motion. The paralysis that impaired my vision was a rare thing even for the Warm Springs doctors who treated thousands of polio patients. They sent me by ambulance to a LaGrange eye doctor who prescribed that I wear an eye patch to eliminate the double vision and exercise my eyes as much as I could. The patch reduced the scope of my vision and eliminated depth perception. Eventually, my brain took over the function of the patch, and I could see satisfactorily by subconsciously accepting only one image transmitted to my brain by my eyes. I had sensation all over my body and could feel a touch, but I had no muscular response. Somehow I kept expecting that I would wake up some day to find my arms or legs twitching, and gradually motion would return. There were no such awakenings.

It would be impossible to evaluate the therapeutic benefits of a place like Warm Springs. The gracious, white brick buildings were tucked away amid beautiful, towering trees. Red clay roads curved back from the highway through the timber, opening onto the cluster of buildings. The whole place had a special feeling of sanctuary. The staff, composed of many local people related to one another, provid-ed a sense of family. Even the winter had been gentle and rainy. To an Illinois native, the subtlety of the Georgia spring was fascinating. It crept over the land, leaving dots of dogwood blossoms and beds of early tulips. All of this contributed to the special peace and serenity of the place.

There was also a spiritual quality to the healing. With such ex-cellent care my mental attitude improved. There was much joy amidst so much destruction. People were nice to each other, and friendships were forged that I still cherish today. In the midst of those well-ordered surroundings, I began to believe that I could accom-modate to my much-altered physical self. The awakening land and the approach of Easter paralleled the feeling that there would be life after polio.

> There is a balm in Gilead,
> To make the wounded whole;
> There is a balm in Gilead,
> To heal the sin-sick soul.

I sang "The Holy City" in church on Palm Sunday, a prelude to an exciting week. Dad was coming. I know how badly I wanted to see him, but my longing couldn't compare to Mother's. She needed to talk to him. The DePlaces, who lived in the front apartment with their grandchildren while their daughter was a patient, had been wonderful to Mother; but they could only help the loneliness. She had deep concerns to share with Dad. Miss Wilson, my therapist, had been easing Mother into the grim reality of my future although I didn't know it. We waited for the beautiful April days to pass quickly.

Dad would be coming in our new "used" Buick that he had bought. He would stop first in Kentucky on business and would leave after Easter for Carolina before going home. Plans were to take me to Mother's apartment where she would cook me anything I wanted to perk up my appetite. She was discouraged that my weight had only climbed to 88 pounds. I had asked for waffles, so tucked in with Dad's luggage and briefcase would be the waffle iron. Dad was probably hungry for Mother's cooking, too, but he more likely wanted a pot roast or meat loaf.

We hoped he would arrive on Thursday, but he was there Tuesday night already. He and Mother came for all my treatments, and he took Mother around to the tourist areas.

Although Dad was strong and could easily lift me into the roomy four-door car, I still did not fold up into a very compact unit. My neck muscles were so weak that I could not hold my head up in a moving car, so Mother had to sit behind me to provide support. This was long before the days of car headrests, and when my head would fall backwards, I could not pick it up again. My own wheelchair arrived that Friday, and since it was collapsible, Dad took me to Manchester on my first shopping trip. I bought a yellow dress for Easter, trimmings for a hat to enter in a contest, and remembrances for people back home.

Easter itself was a glorious day, and the chapel was filled with visitors. My roommate Bev's parents from Ohio were also visiting. I sang that night at fellowship hour and won first place with my purple hat with its egg nest on top. All too soon the visit was over, and Dad had to leave for his next appointment.

Dad often traveled during the months Mother and I were gone. When not on the road, he commuted to Chicago daily, leaving at 6:45 A.M. and returning at 6:20 P.M. if the train was on time. How strange it must have seemed to him, alone in the big house that used to bustle with four busy people. How depressing to return to a darkened, empty house with no supper until he cooked it himself, yet he never complained.

My treatments at the foundation continued. I could stand in the pool for 70 unsteady seconds. I was fitted with long leg braces just for exercise purposes as my arms and shoulders could not handle crutches. I had learned to turn to one side in bed and was learning to read lying on my side. In late May when Dad's business was to take him to Florida, he picked up Mother to accompany him for a well-earned vacation. She cleared the apartment to return home with him, confident that I would receive good care.

Not long after that, the doctors dismissed me and said I could return home. The news was both welcome and distressing. Of course, I wanted to go home, but I was not well. I could not walk or use either hand. Perhaps my confusion, though unspoken, registered on the clinic staff. Perhaps a dismissal lecture from the physical therapist was standard practice. I really don't know, but one brilliant June morning she took me outside in my wheelchair. We stopped under the beautiful colonnades. At the other end of the sloped lawn the usual morning traffic moved back and forth along the medical building porch — nurses, pushboys moving patients to or from therapy, housekeeping staff, and others. A few patients with their therapists were practicing walking on the paved court.

Miss Wilson and I were alone in the cool early morning, rather apart from it all. She was serious and tried to be kind, but her message was brutal. *I was not going to get any better!* She gave me the facts. Those muscles that hadn't returned in the first months after the onset were not going to return. I had not responded to therapy. They had fitted me with arm slings and hand splints, but there was nothing more I could gain from staying at Warm Springs. In fact, I was taking a bed some other person needed. They had done as much as they could.

I sat mutely with tears streaming down my face, tears that I could not even wipe away. I did not cry out or tell her she was wrong, but I knew she was. She had to be. I had always recovered before, no matter how sick I had been. Besides, being a cripple for the rest of my life would be too unfair. I didn't deserve that severe a punishment. Someday I'd walk back to this place and look her up and show her how wrong she was. She couldn't hear my thoughts, but she might have guessed them. She was telling me not to expect a miracle. I would have to make the best of it as I was, and I should not make life miserable for others just because I was crippled. It was a harsh message.

Our God, Our Help in Ages Past

My parents must have been as startled as I to receive the news that I was dismissed and could return home. They were hardly back from their brief Florida business/vacation trip when I called them long distance to relay my news. I'm sure Mother had dug right into cleaning when she arrived home, as the house had been more or less neglected in her absence. Dad had dusted, washed, and done the necessary weekly tasks, but he had certainly not done a spring cleaning. This was a ritual with Mother, and I suspect she was deep in the midst of it when she realized I would be home.

She and Dad made all the arrangements. They took down the dining room table and brought my double bed downstairs, since it would be impossible to carry me up and down stairs whenever I needed to lie down. There would be room for my wheelchair in the large living room, and I could eat on my lapboard in the kitchen doorway. The worst factor was that the only bathroom was upstairs, and there was no space to install one on the first floor. The arrangements were far from the best, but we would once again be together as a family.

Dad flew to Atlanta to meet me and accompany me home on a return flight. The foundation staff did all my packing for me — a task they accomplished with the skill of experience. I was delivered to the Atlanta airport by ambulance and carried on board the plane. Dad was there waiting. I was able to sit in a passenger seat in a reclining position during the flight home, and Dad could shift my position occasionally. In Chicago Uncle Clyde and Mother were waiting with the ambulance for the trip home. My suitcases (which had been gifts from the Sunday school), wheelchair, lapboard, and assorted parcels were packed in around me.

My doctor had characterized me as a "pathetic case," and the foundation labeled me "helpless," but my parents were determined to handle my care themselves. Mother was experienced in caring for me over the years, and she had been given instructions at Warm Springs for my home therapy program. She had also been trained to transfer me from bed to wheelchair or vice versa without physically picking me up as Dad did. I was unaware until years later that an uncle had told my parents never to bring me home again because of my severe limitations. He told them to leave me at Warm Springs or they would be saddled with me for life. He seemed to comprehend what Miss Wilson had been trying to tell me, but he underestimated the devotion of my parents. There was never any question in their minds that they could manage with the help of God. They welcomed me home and committed the rest of their lives to me. Their prayers echoed the words of the hymn:

> Our God, our Help in ages past,
> Our Hope for years to come.

I wish I could say that the adjustment was smooth and easy, but, of course, it wasn't. At first I could not even turn in the soft, double bed, and it seemed Mother would never get her rest if she had to come downstairs during the night and change my position to prevent bed sores. Second, the bed was low for Mother when she worked on me, especially when she went through my therapy routine two or three times a day. Both problems were solved when we borrowed a hospital bed on a free loan, with the condition that Dad would paint and fix it up. He also built a frame above it to suspend the pulleys used for my leg exercises. So that I would not always be imprisoned in the house, Dad built a long ramp from the sidewalk up to our front porch. In an emergency or when Dad was away at work or traveled, Mother could get me in or out of the house alone, although pushing me up the ramp was a herculean task.

Visitors were a mixed blessing. Many, many people dropped in, but we appreciated most those who called first to match our schedule. Countless people told me of other polio victims they had known who had also been totally paralyzed, but who had been determined they would walk again, had never given up, and now walked. I know their intentions were good. They truly meant to encourage me, but they implied that I was not trying. I tried to be polite and praise the victor, but I silently resented these success stories.

I'm sure most people thought that the few hours they visited me were especially good for Mother, as she would sit down during that time. This was probably true, but few recognized that Mother was fulfilling several jobs — wife, mother, cook, cleaning lady, laundress, therapist, and full-time nurse for an invalid. What she needed most was an occasional helping hand, but none was given. No one ever ironed one of the fresh shirts Dad wore daily, washed one window, changed one bed, cleaned one room, or gave me one bit of personal care. Many did bring food gifts, which were always appreciated. Mother usually did more than her share of the entertaining because many people thought it would be easier to come to our house than to get me somewhere else.

Mother always had marvelous organizational ability, and she kept schedules that would have exhausted nearly anyone else. She really should have had some hired help, but she was always too conscious of the cost. Unlike some polio patients, whose costs for either housekeeping or nursing staff at home were paid by charitable organizations, I received no further help. We were more than grateful for what we had received, and we began saving our money for a new house all on one floor.

Surprisingly, time did not hang heavy for me. I was able to turn the pages of a book or magazine placed on my lapboard, and I learned to enjoy reading even with double vision. That summer we also bought our first television set. I could watch the Kate Smith show in the living room while Mother listened as she prepared dinner in the kitchen. Friends my age visited once or twice, but their awkwardness matched my own, and we found nothing in common in our different worlds. All but one dropped away completely, but younger neighborhood children, for whom I had baby-sat, visited often and loved to have me tell them stories. They often brought their own show-and-tell. As I lay on my side in bed resting one afternoon, Mother answered the doorbell and admitted Francie bearing a tin can. She promptly marched around the bed and dumped the contents right in front of my nose — a few leaves and a lovely, fat, brown and black caterpillar. These little friends filled many empty hours that first summer back home.

Ours was certainly an altered life-style. It was not impossible, but there were frustations. Polio had converted me into a *former* perfectionist. I couldn't forget my father's teaching that the job worth doing was worth doing well. His projects took a long time but were done well. I began to practice working with my hand splint, trying to gain control of the few muscles left in my right arm and shoulder. Writing was shaky and slow, but it began to improve. I commandeered Dad's old portable typewriter from the closet. It was not nearly as easy to use as the IBM electric that I had tried in therapy, but it never repeated a letter if I was slow. It was hard to strike the keys evenly with the inverted pencil, but I began to develop the accuracy I would need to complete high school courses. Since I could not sit up in a wheelchair for very long at a time, I seldom completed a letter in one sitting. In fact, a two page letter could take all day with rest periods and therapy in between. My lack of strength constantly slowed me, and my desire to get better and stronger burned within me.

During those early weeks at home I developed a secret for living with my handicap. I decided never to complain about it, at least not out loud to any human. Very early I seemed to understand the futility of complaints and the sadness they brought to those who heard them. I also decided never to say, "I wish I could," about anything that was impossible because of my handicap. That would only make those around me feel helpless, too. Thus, I could complain if I was tired due to a cold (everyone gets that feeling), but never if I was tired because my back muscles were too weak to support me. I could say that I wished I could read some book (because that was physically possible), but never that I wished I could play the piano again (although I did). When I began the game of pretending that my limitations did not really bother me and of never admitting my secret frustrations, I did not expect that it would last so long.

I guess I continued to wait for my miracle healing. I took comfort that God's strength is made perfect in weakness, yet I continued to believe that mine was only a temporary weakness. I loved the following anonymous verse, which I discovered could be sung to the melody of "Blessed Assurance." This version suited my feelings.

> God hath not promised skies always blue,
> Flower-strewn pathways all my life through;
> God hath not promised sun without rain,
> Joy without sorrow, peace without pain.
>
> But God hath promised strength for the day,
> Rest from the labor, light for the way,
> Grace for the trials, help from above,
> Unending mercy, undying love.

About this time a church friend gave me a copy of a book of Alice Hansche Mortenson's verses. The title poem "I Needed the Quiet" with its explanation of sickness seemed to speak to me directly, especially the first stanza.

> I needed the quiet so He drew me aside
> Into the shadows where we could confide
> Away from the bustle where all the day long
> I hurried and worried when active and strong.

There was no doubt that I needed the quiet. Secretly and silently I might be rebelling, but in my heart I knew I was bearing the cross I had prayed would bring me closer to God. I hope I accepted it with as good grace as possible. I know that with the constant love and support of my parents I began to pick up the pieces of my shattered life and set some reasonable goals for myself. The first objective seemed to be to get a high school education. After all, my body had atrophied, not my mind. Everyone else my age was thinking of returning to school in September, and I too wondered about my education.

Believe, Believe

Back to school! Those words used to herald the best part of my summer, for I loved school. I was always eager to return, meet my new teachers, try the new work, and pick up again with friends. This year, however, would be different. Becoming crippled had changed my educational status. I was no longer a regular student under the guidance of a school principal and staff. I was no longer eligible to attend school. Instead, I was under the direction of the Child Study Department and would be tutored at home.

Actually, this was not really too disappointing to me. I knew from those few visits from my peers during the summer that our lives were so different that friendship would be strained. I also knew that the maximum time I could sit up in my wheelchair was less than two hours. School would last a lot longer than that. Also, the building where I would attend was an older structure, and getting from class to class would be difficult.

My joy was great when I learned that one of my favorite teachers from junior high school was to be my tutor. He would come each night after school for one hour and teach me all subjects. I would study alone on my own time. Each afternoon at about 3:45 Mother would be sure that I was up in my wheelchair or sitting on the sofa ready for "school." A card table and chair were always ready for the teacher, and my books and completed assignments all laid out.

It never occurred to me that school would be hard. It had always been so easy. I had seldom felt challenged in any school subject. But I had never been crippled before. I had always delighted in special projects that allowed me to combine my drawing ability with writing or research. Now writing was slow and difficult. This was before the days of felt-tipped pens, and I did not have enough pressure to bear down on a ballpoint pen. I resorted to an ink pen that frequently

57

smudged or left unwanted blots on my work. My pencil writing was very light due to that same lack of pressure. My reading was manageable, although turning pages quickly and holding books open were new problems that tested my patience. Coupled with these problems was my choice of subjects—two in particular. I had received the highest grade on the eighth grade language aptitude test in Esperanto, so I elected German with high confidence. Mathematics had always been easy, so algebra was sure to be a cinch. I cite these factors as I must take my share of the blame for what happened.

My tutor had known me as a quick, eager student. I'm sure he was unprepared for my altered abilities. Also, he had been promoted to grade school principal that year, and the responsibilities of his new job often made him late. A few minutes made no difference, but when he came as much as 45 minutes late, I was impatient and already quite tired. I felt that he never really prepared any lessons for me and only looked at the books after he arrived. When I began to have trouble with both algebra and German, my frustration soared. I, who had never earned anything but an A, found myself with unwanted B's. I couldn't understand why I wasn't learning as before, and in desperation I blamed the teacher whom I had once adored. One spring evening I recklessly dared to ask a bold question.

"Do you ever look at the books before you come?"

He too must have been dissatisfied with our progress, for he was quick to respond, "If you want a teacher who reads the books, I'll get you one." With that he closed his books and got up and left.

My chest felt constricted, and my heart was pounding. I was stunned. What had I done? I knew I was never to show disrespect to a teacher. What would Mother say? She was already heading in from the kitchen and asking why he had left early. But she was not angry with me. She had known how hard the tardiness had been for me, and she knew how faithfully I tried each day to do and understand my lessons and how hurt I was to get the B grades.

We never heard from him again. The next day the director of the Child Study Department called to say that Mrs. Fletcher, a regular homebound tutor, would be coming to teach me. I have no idea what he gave as his reason for quitting. I know that we were never offered a chance either to explain or to apologize. I also know now that the Lord was working in my life for good, for Mrs. Fletcher and I worked well together. Because tutoring was her only job, she could come in the early afternoon before I became tired. She finished the year for me. The director of the department advised me to forget about a second year of German. Reluctantly, I agreed, although I hated to be a quitter. Mrs. Fletcher expected my best effort, and I gave it.

During this time Dad had been designing a new house for us.

He worked long hours each night over his drawing board making the complete construction plans for a smaller house all on one floor. When he was finished, he took his set of drawings to a contractor for an estimate of the cost. It was more than we could afford, much more.

Literally, Dad went back to the drawing board. We agreed to cut back to a one-car garage and eliminate a second bathroom and third bedroom. Along with new plans Dad found another cost-cutting measure. He would serve as his own general contractor during the construction.

Earl Hageman and his son undertook the carpenter work, cement work, and on-site supervision. Another friend laid the bricks. Dad engaged good tradesmen whom he respected for the plumbing, heating, and electrical work. He did as much of the work himself as he could. An excavating crew began digging the basement that summer. This arrangement worked for us, since we could not sell our home until the new house was ready for occupancy. Families with an invalid could not just pick up and find temporary quarters, we felt, so we needed to stay where we were.

Mrs. Fletcher returned as my tutor for the sophomore year. I elected general business, geography, and geometry despite my previous frustrations with algebra. My brother had excelled in mathematics and won honors when he graduated. I felt I redeemed myself a bit by loving geometry. It took me hours to work with a compass and protractor, but I drew circles and bisected angles with endless patience. The bookkeeping and check writing for the business course were also slow for me as I labored with a fountain pen. However, I did well in all four subjects, including the required English, and won a Rotary Award for straight A's all year.

Mrs. Stewart had continued to come once a week for my private vocal lessons. One night a week Dad took me to church for choir practice, as I had rejoined the choir. My studies were filled with variety and my days with activity, including the therapy sessions that Mother gave me. Through all of the days ran the excitement of the new house.

Dad spent long hours at work commuting daily to Chicago. Mother would have dinner ready each night. He would quickly eat, change clothes, and go to the house to work until darkness forced him home. After Earl had the house framed up and closed in, Mother and I sometimes went with him for a few hours on weekends. Mother gathered all the wood scraps for the fireplace, and I watched. He sealed the foundation before backfilling. He took down trees and stacked wood for the fireplace.

During the winter Dad began the insulating, fitting bats into every tiny space and making ours the warmest, snuggest house I know. He lathed. He sealed every piece of trim wood on all sides before it was put up and trimmed parts himself. He laid hardwood floors. Besides all this, he supervised the work of his subcontractors. It took longer to build this way, but it is a well-built house that has served us well.

At the beginning of my junior year we moved in. Only my bedroom and the bathroom were decorated. The rest of the walls were bare white plaster. Nothing in the yard was done except the rough grading. There were many fine touches still to complete, but the house was marvelously convenient and compact. The rest could be finished over the years as we lived there.

The same weekend we moved into our house, Dad's business moved out of Chicago. It became necessary for him to drive each day to the new location. This cut some minutes off his day away from home, but it meant he could no longer relax on the train. Our church moved at the same time from the low, mission church into a new gothic structure. Everywhere were stairs—two to the outside door, eight more inside at the most convenient door. There was no place in the sanctuary for a wheelchair except in one of the aisles. Choir practice meant going down a long flight of stairs to the basement after first coming up outside steps to the door. From that time on activities at church meant my father had to steady the wheelchair on its big back wheels and drag/roll me in it up or down stairs. Occasionally, such as when I sang for funerals and the undertakers took me, others did this balancing maneuver, but almost exclusively Dad assumed the responsibility. He preferred to do it alone to preserve his balance on the narrow stair treads. I closed my eyes and counted the bump of each step up and down.

The inconvenient church created certain problems. My parents never considered attending church without me or staying home, but we did think about changing churches. However, attending an accessible church would have meant changing our denominational affiliation, so we stayed with our home church until Dad entered his eightieth year. Then we transferred to the daughter congregation with its new, barrier-free sanctuary.

In addition to a new home, office, and church, my school routine was about to change, too. Mrs. Fletcher had decided not to teach me again. My studies were getting more complex and required too much preparation time for her. Instead, a regular teacher from each high school class would come one day a week and teach me his subject specialty. Mrs. Fletcher could have continued once a week with my English, for example, but she decided it was better that I have a change before we both went stale. How wise of her. Our time together had been good. Perhaps she understood homebound students better, or perhaps she had no preconceived expectations when she came. I was different too—older, stronger, and wiser. I suspect it was God working things together for good, for we both loved God.

Different teachers were an uplifting change. I had been able to elect art, and a marvelous man dragged paints, boards, clay, and all sorts of materials to the house to broaden my concepts about art. A perky, dedicated lady who loved young people as well as her subject taught me to love biology. Under her guidance, I raced through the course completing a year's work in just over one semester. Once more I used my drawing skills to illustrate simple plant and animal structures. A lovely, sensitive lady encouraged my creative writing in her English class and stretched my writing skills. Her reading poetry to me with tears in her eyes shaped some of my poetry tastes for life.

The year began, however, with one unresolved problem. No one from the American history department was free or willing to give up an hour after school each week to tutor me. For a while it looked as if the failure to fulfill that requirement would keep me from completing my junior year. Then the head of the school system's radio station, a former history teacher himself, volunteered to do the teaching. What a wonderful year it was, and once again I won the Rotary Award for straight A's.

My senior year was to be handled the same way, but again a few snags occurred. A social studies teacher could be found for only one semester — the social problems course required for graduation — but he was a super teacher. He forced me to think and examine my own values. He then solved the problem of a second semester teacher by offering to teach the economics course himself. Another outstanding English teacher came, subconsciously shaping my future. The new art teacher was a genius, patiently teaching me techniques of both water colors and oils.

The state required credits in physical education for graduation. Obviously, I could not do push-ups or play volleyball, but a tutor was hired who would come Monday evenings. She had been my mother's teacher in high school and was a friend of our friends. Also, she was totally undaunted by the state's requirements.

The first night she arrived carrying a stack of eight or ten health books. As she handed them to Mother, she must have noted the look on my face.

"Don't worry, You don't have to read them all. Just read something from each one by the end of the year."

"I can do that," I said.

"I thought tonight we'd play a game," she suggested, pulling a box from her carryall. "Chinese checkers! Do you know how to play?"

"Not very well," I confessed. Some years earlier I had played a game or two. I could certainly try.

I'm afraid our efforts at gamesmanship were more trying for the teacher. The game was an unfortunate, though funny, choice. I, who could not pinch my fingers together to pick up a marble, tried the next best thing — to nudge them across the board. Sometimes my nudges went a bit out of control, sending a minor avalanche of marbles rolling. Just slightly before I'd lost all my marbles, a bolt of pure inspiration struck the teacher.

"Do you play bridge?" she asked.

"No, but I'd like to."

"Then that's what we'll do," she said, packing up her marbles to go home. "Starting next week, we play bridge." Play bridge we did. I already had a set of wooden card racks to hold the cards. Mother joined us, as she knew how to play, and various friends were drafted as fourths. Of course, I could neither shuffle nor deal, but I did learn enough to play a game that has brought me hours of enjoyment, to say nothing of meeting the state's requirement.

My biggest disappointment was the class I looked forward to the most — journalism. The school newspaper sponsor taught this, and, though I liked her, I certainly misunderstood her course work. One day she asked me to type a chart of correction symbols for her. Since all her lessons for me were in longhand, I concluded she couldn't or didn't type. I assumed this was a favor for her personally, which I would gladly do, but I decided to save it for summer to have time for neatness and accuracy. She never mentioned it again until she asked for it the last session. Too late I realized my error and tried to explain. She dismissed my excuses and said I would have to take a zero.

While I was still reeling in dismay, she began orally giving me a glossary of terms she said I would need to know for the final exam. I couldn't take notes fast enough, so I tried to remember. My mind was too numb; never had I skipped any assigned work before. My course grade was a *B,* and I missed my coveted Rotary Award because of that one grade.

I never really felt part of the school life. I did write some for the school newspaper in the journalism class, but I never worked with any staff member. The yearbook sponsor invited me to join her staff, but again I wrote alone at home. I was physically at the school only two days. In my junior year the radio station director (who was teaching me American history) arranged for me to visit for a day. He lifted me in and out of his car and took me into the school at the loading dock. Students pushed me from class to class. It was a wonderful idea, but physically exhausting. So many students and teachers spoke to me; so much was going on. By early afternoon I had a headache and felt woozy. The teacher had to take me home before the end of the school day. I realized what little stamina I actually possessed.

The other time I was present was for the Honors Day assembly in my senior year. I had been asked to sing a solo. I was also graduating in the top 20 and was to receive honors in English and a pin for working on the yearbook. Two days before the assembly, my economics tutor realized that I was eligible for honors in social studies too, having all A's for six semesters.

I wore a cap and gown like the rest of the class, but felt a certain anxiety because I was the only handicapped senior. The song selected by my voice teacher was a difficult number. Well over a thousand people were in the gym as I sang,

> I talked to God last night,
> Begged Him my doubts to relieve,
> And as night turned to day, I heard a voice say,
> "Believe, believe!"

Being a graduating senior was exciting. My picture appeared in the newspaper receiving the first copy of the yearbook from the class president at the Honors Day program. Mail came from friends and relatives. Many gave gifts, including some local merchants. The high school gym was sweltering the night of graduation, but I can't even remember being warm. The head custodian pushed my wheelchair down the center aisle as the class marched down the outside aisles to "Pomp and Circumstance." A neighbor of ours was president of the Board of Education, and it was a special moment when he presented me my diploma. After graduation, my closest friend had invited the entire graduating class of 370 to a garden party at her home, and most of us went. My parents hosted a family party for me the following day. Graduation marked the first goal. The future seemed uncertain, but Jesus had said to take no thought for the morrow.

The high school years had sped by. During that time Dad had changed jobs and joined a small, family-owned engineering firm, once more commuting into Chicago each day. A former associate of Dad's had joined the firm earlier and persuaded Dad to join, too. Together they would have the first option to buy the firm when the owners retired. Bill was much younger than Dad, but they worked well together. It was a great opportunity for Dad.

Well-meaning friends had also persuaded my parents that I should see some other doctors, since I was obviously getting no better. We felt the Warm Springs experience had been the best available; still it seemed ungrateful to ignore their recommendations of a Chicago specialist who had reportedly done so much for post-polios with exercise and injections. He promised nothing but encouraged us to try his program. He hinted darkly, though, that we had waited too long. His best results were within the first year.

The injections were to be given in the arm with a hypodermic syringe. Mother, who had found no aspect of my care too revolting to perform, said she could not jab the needle into my toothpick arms. A nurse friend taught Dad the technique. After his practice shots on an orange he began on me. His was a steady hand, and rarely did I have any bruising.

Along with home exercises I had to go to the doctor's private clinic in Winnetka monthly. There therapists put me through more strenuous exercises and stretching. I was taught to fall out of my wheelchair onto a mat. In my long leg braces I was hoisted upright between parallel bars and inched along a six-foot course with help in front and behind. During my senior year I went on Saturday mornings. After school was out, I went for a seven-hour day. Dad drove me to the clinic, caught the train across the street for his work, came back early, and drove me home again in midafternoon.

It became obvious that we were too late. Although it was probably good for me to be moved about so vigorously, I was not making any physical improvement. After a fair trial period, my parents discussed how best to terminate the program.

In late August I had my first asthma attack—a terrifying experience for us all. Although I was gasping for each shallow breath, I had no feeling that I was dying. Panic swept my parents, and they called Dr. Partridge. It was a Wednesday, and he was out of town at his brother-in-law's fishing. Mother instucted Dad to go across the street for our psychiatrist neighbor, Dr. Lieberman, who had recently moved in. He came at once, a marvelously calming man who gave me a mild sedative. Nonetheless, he went back home almost at once to use his own connections to reach Dr. Partridge with the message to come home quickly.

While he was gone, Mother asked, "Do you want us to call Pastor Schuth?"

"No," I told her. "I'm not dying."

My breathing performance must have been most unconvincing, for she sent Dad across the street to use a neighbor's phone and call him anyway. In the meantime Dr. Lieberman casually came back to sit with me for a while. I had no idea Dr. Partridge had been summoned and was on the way. I actually would not have cared anyway, as the sedative and Dr. Lieberman's soothing manner were beginning to lull me to a gasping sleep.

Dad was back from the Smiths', although I hadn't known he'd been there. The Smiths had begun to pray for me. He whispered to Mother that Pastor Schuth was in a Sunday school teachers' meeting, but was coming at once. He paused only long enough to alert the meeting to pray for me. Suddenly he was at my bedside. It wasn't all quite connecting in my mind. I had said not to call him. Had he dropped in? I listened to his prayer and slurred along with him on the Lord's Prayer as my speech had become a bit thick.

Both Pastor Schuth and Dr. Lieberman were among the welcoming committee when Dr. Partridge drove up a remarkably short time later considering the distance he had come. He deftly gave me a shot of adrenalin. Within minutes my breathing had eased, and the heavy compression on my chest seemed lifted. The labor of breathing and the sedative combined, and I slept briefly. When I awoke, every sense was heightened. I was unaware then that asthma had become a part of my life.

Searching for a reason for the asthma attack, my parents decided that my seven-hour therapy sessions had worn me down. I had been trying too hard. As I was anxious to start college, we all agreed to discontinue the other treatments. I didn't seem strong enough for both, and the one was obviously not helping. Perhaps college would.

College had always been a goal. Becoming crippled had not dimmed the desire. If anything, it had become stronger. It was obvious, if I hoped to support myself, that I would have to use brains instead of brawn. The idea of becoming a teacher was growing in my mind.

One of my high school tutors had inquired if I intended taking any of the tests to try for any scholarships. When I consulted the director of the Child Study Department, she assured me my education would be taken care of. Our school system at that time included a two-year community college. She said my tuition, which was minimal, would be paid through her department. If I applied for a scholarship and won, I would be taking it away from someone else whose college expenses were not already guaranteed as mine were. Being a scholarship winner would have been a feather in my cap, but not competing (or needing to) was such an easy solution. I felt that I personally was giving someone else a chance at college. How noble of me! How smug!

I should have been more suspicious of that woman and tried to protect my own interests better. All along she had counseled that college was really unnecessary for me anyway. She had advised me not to pursue the second year of German nor any other language. The handwriting was on the wall, but I was letting my rosy lenses obscure my vision.

Continuing my education at the local college had some decided advantages. Since the college shared staff and space with the high school, I felt some faculty would already know me. I wouldn't be a stranger. Also, I could continue to live at home and receive my parents' care. I could still sing in the church choir. I could keep my little job maintaining the mailing list for the Easter Seal association. I really didn't have good enough control to post donations in the tiny marked boxes on the index cards, but Mother did that part for me. I did all the typing of new cards and made the changes of address weekly.

The college ran day and evening classes. Both options posed problems with transportation. Before any details were worked out, the child study director intervened with an interesting alternative.

She mentioned a new communications system which operated over leased telephone wires that allowed a student at home to hear everything that went on in a classroom miles away. By depressing a bar on the home unit, which was about the size of a small adding machine, the student could respond to questions and participate in class. The companion unit in the classroom was portable and could be moved from class to class by unplugging it from the special telephone jack and plugging it in again where the next class was held. The initial costs for installing jacks and the monthly rate for leased wires would all be paid for me. It would be just a matter of selecting courses that the college would schedule in convenient rooms.

Everyone was willing to cooperate, and I liked the idea of being a student from home. This method would permit me to "attend" classes even on days when I wasn't well enough to get out of bed. The only problem might be in getting my papers back and forth. Mother didn't drive, and Dad was out of town long before the school office opened. Our good neighbors, the Scharfs, solved this. Al was a teacher in the high school. He offered to provide courier service for me. Mother would take my finished work across the street as he left for school in the morning. When he checked his own school mailbox first thing, he would put my papers in the appropriate teacher's box. Work for me was left in Al's box, and Becky would bring it to me when her daddy came home from school. Tests were sometimes sent by mail, and my papers were often returned in batches, so this was not an excessive strain on them. Since Mother and I were nearly always home, our house became the place where Becky came after school when her mother wasn't home. That made us feel we were doing something in return for their help.

The best plan was for me to "attend" day classes with one night course so I could mix somewhat with fellow students. The program had to be approved by Dr. Partridge—the first snag. He would only approve two-thirds of a semester, not the full load. "That would mean three years to complete two years of junior college!" I protested.

"Exactly!"

"But I've been taking a full year in high school."

"College is different," he said. "You'll have more reading, which is hard for you. And college papers are longer and take more time. What's your hurry anyway?" He was being so reasonable.

Everyone agreed with him. My health was more important than speed. It was implied that I wasn't going anywhere. Maybe I wasn't; I didn't know. I really had no choice, but I picked subjects carefully for English and social studies majors. I was thinking of subjects I might be able to teach.

Beginning college was exciting. Lecture classes worked well on the Executone school-to-home unit. Unfortunately, when I depressed the bar to speak, I could hear nothing in class. Parts of my responses would become lost if I was not steady, but I wouldn't know this until I released the bar and the teacher would ask me to repeat. I discovered the best method was to hold the bar with my elbow and lean on it. Once in a while the students responsible for transferring the school unit would forget to do so or be absent. I would turn on my unit at home and hear nothing, except a stray ham operator now and then. Mother would quickly call the school office where someone would be dispatched at once to get the unit and plug me in. But this happened rarely.

I took the English requirements, speech, survey courses in literature, and history courses by this method. The fabulous art teacher I had in my senior year of high school held Saturday seminars for his really dedicated students to come in to work. He included me in these, picking me up each Saturday morning and returning me at noon. What wonderful sessions these were with his best students there to lend me a hand with my projects. I painted, enameled copper, constructed a miniature room, and earned credits in design. These were among my best class sessions, although they made painfully clear how limited my artistic abilities had become. I longed for the sure hand and keen eyesight of my childhood that would never be again.

Midway through my second year I encountered a problem when one instructor refused to have a student in class he could not see. Until then, no one had questioned whether I would or could cheat at home, and I had never violated the trust shown me. Indeed, the B's that I had hated so in high school became fairly common, but I would never cheat for an A. Did he fear cheating?

Not being accepted was a new crisis. The teacher wanted to see me if I was to be in his class. Since his course was also offered evenings, I enrolled in that section instead, knowing Dad would take me to classes. I had just about exhausted the courses that would work well over the school-to-home unit anyway, at least the ones that offered credits to transfer to a four-year college later. Leasing the phone wire for one class seemed an unnecessary expense, so I transferred fully to the night school program. This seemed to terminate my association with the Child Study Department, something I think the director had wanted for a long time. I assumed all my college expenses myself. Fortunately, they weren't high.

I wish I could say that the teacher who refused me in class because he could not see me finally accepted me and learned to like me, but that was not so. I realize now that this was the first discrimination I faced, but I didn't recognize it at the time.

I made a friend in class, a young secretary named Irene. We studied together and compared grades, usually only a few points apart. If mine were higher, I felt it was because I had time to read more thoroughly, although Irene wrote fluently and could express herself better on essay tests. Our last book was *Moby Dick,* which Irene just didn't find time to read. When we reviewed for the test, I told her the story as I understood it.

Most of that final was based on *Moby Dick,* but I didn't have time to worry about Irene as I struggled to hurry with my erratic backhand. When the final grades came, Irene had an *A* for the course and I a *B.* As with my high school journalism grade, I felt an injustice had been done. This time I decided to do something about it.

I made an appointment to see the teacher. Dad took me to his room and left. In a minute the teacher arrived. I was very careful with what I said because I didn't want Irene's grade to be lowered. "I wondered if there was a mistake in my final grade," I began.

"Oh, I don't think so," he oozed and opened his grade book to show me.

I pointed to my good grades in the course and casually compared them to Irene's a few lines away. "My grades almost match Irene's."

He knew we were friends and had probably compared grades. "Yes," he smiled, "but the difference was the final. Irene's was far better than yours."

"Could I see my final?" I asked. The finals had not been returned.

"I'm sorry," he said, "but I didn't save them after I graded them."

"I thought finals had to be kept on file for a semester."

"Not here, they don't. It's a matter of teacher preference. I prefer not to keep them." He held all the trump cards, and he knew it. He decided to throw me a kindness. "I hope you're not discouraged. You did very well, considering."

Considering I'm crippled, I thought, but I said nothing. There was no way I could prove or be shown who was right. It was like trying to nail down shadows. Seething with anger, I waited for Dad to return. Hot tears stung my eyes, but there was nothing I could do. Even if I went to the dean, my case was hopeless with no finals to compare as evidence. I had to accept whatever grade he gave me.

As much as I burned over the experience and regretted taking his course, I eventually had a satisfying revelation: Irene had not read much of the book, but with my tutoring she had done well on the test. I could teach!

The family of my childhood

Four years later, my fifth grade picture

Sonny in fifth grade

My confirmation

Summer of '49—My last piano recital
(not wearing glasses to look glamorous)

Summer of '49—
Sonny's high school
graduation picture

Mary at the piano

Sharing his dad's love of cars, Sonny willingly waxed the family car.

Iron lung slightly opened to show the cot for the patient

At Warm Springs (where patients were dressed each day) with lapboard, overhead arm slings, and handsplints

Dad, who arrived early in Holy Week, with Mother and me at Warm Springs Foundation [picture by Louis Baer, my roommate' father]

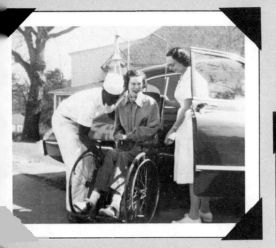

Being lifted into the car at Warm Springs for my first ride since polio

My own new wheelchair and new dress after my first shopping trip (my weight was up to about 80 pounds by then)

Leaving chapel services Easter Sunday—Dad is pushing me, and Mother is on the grass with Mrs. Baer

Daily Courier News photo

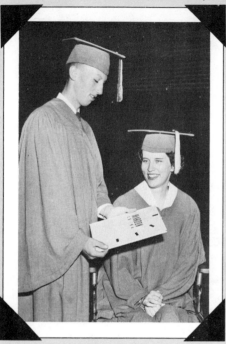

At Honor's Day receiving the first yearbook
from the class president, Bob Gillam

School-to-home unit that allowed me to listen
and talk to college classes from home over
leased telephone lines

Daily Courier News photo

Daily Courier News photo

Receiving Easter Seal Gallantry Award from my principal,
Ross Hulmes, March 1963

Receiving award at Warm Springs from Basil O'Connor, President F. D. Roosevelt's law partner, November 1964

Publicity photo provided by Warm Springs Foundation

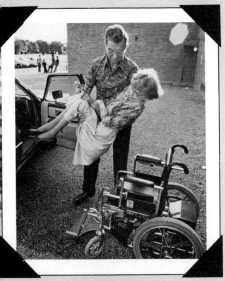

Arriving at school

Photo © 1983 by David Tonge.

Photo © 1983 by David Tonge.

Still teaching after twenty-two years—Jennifer confers on a paper.

Photo © 1983 by David Tonge.

Becky and Rich load the computer for a special project.

Great Is
Thy Faithfulness

As my junior college experience progressed, I became desperate for another school at which to finish my work and earn a degree. I had first written to the University of Illinois in the summer of 1955 but had never received any answer. This school was my first choice, as we had heard that the program there was the finest in the world for handicapped students. Although we were no longer under the director of the Child Study Department since I was paying my own college expenses, we again contacted the director for advice and help. She referred me to the State Division of Vocational Rehabilitation, which, she assured me, would help me complete my education and perhaps even help me obtain a job. I was eligible simply because I was handicapped. It seemed too good to be true—and it was.

A counselor came to our house for my first interview. He was neither optimistic nor encouraging, but he said he would be back. He came again, and I found myself forming a dislike for him. He held a certain power over my destiny, and I feared he lacked both the wisdom and compassion to use that power well. Basically, we wanted the department to open doors for us at the University of Illinois so I could get an interview and be accepted as a student. We were willing to pay all our own expenses. I thought I had the right qualifications—a 4.5 junior college average, Illinois residency, and a handicap. I only needed a little help to reach the right people, I thought.

As the counselor talked, it became clear that he didn't think a college education was necessary for me. When he came, he usually had a young man with him who waited in the car. On the first occasion Mother asked if his friend wouldn't prefer to wait inside. He said he was a client and told us that he was on parole after committing numerous crimes and was now being rehabilitated into a job. I think I grew to be jealous of this youth who had been accepted into the program for a second chance at life while I felt I was going to be turned down for help.

Once the counselor looked around our big living room like a real estate appraiser and said that anyone who could live in a house like this did not deserve any help. Of course, we thought our home was special, but it was only four and a half rooms. I thought of the hours of Dad's labor so that we could afford the house. Now it was being held against us. Mother, however, had an answer for him. She reminded him that we were not asking for financial help. He then said I would have to take an IQ test to see if I was eligible. My successful school record would count for nothing.

A date for testing was set, and a different counselor came to administer the test at home. The test was a Wexler-Bellvue, which had large sections of manual dexterity. On the lap board of my wheelchair, he laid out pieces of a puzzle that I could easily see would fit together to make a hand. Then he pressed his stopwatch and told me to assemble them. With only one arm that moved and unable to pick up any piece, I pushed, slid, and nudged the pieces to their right places. He clicked off the watch and recorded the time. I was too naive to realize that this kind of test could be used against me. No one with any sense of fairness would give a cripple a performance test to determine intelligence. Yet sections of the test required timing my physical dexterity.

Fortunately, there were oral sections, too. I rapidly repeated series of numbers in reverse order, supplied vocabulary definitions, and tried to prove myself. Later I found out that despite the unfair test, my composite score was 118—too high to eliminate me from the chance to try college.

I refused to believe that the counselor was working against me, but it was so. From the beginning he had sought excuses that would make me ineligible—from estimating we lived in too nice a house to administering an unfair test. He hammered at me, continuously trying to break my faith in myself.

"What do you think you can do as a teacher?"

"I don't know for sure," I had to admit, "but I could at least tutor. I've done that before."

"I'd need evidence that there were opportunities for tutors," he insisted. "And if you intend to tutor here in Elgin, you gotta show me that you could get a job."

I actually felt that his department was supposed to help me get a job, but it was no time to be picky. I made an appointment with the school superintendent, Orin Thompson, and explained to him my need for assurance that tutoring positions existed.

"Mary," he said, "get all the education you can get. You'll never be sorry."

"But would I be able to use my education as a teacher?" I asked.

"Right now I could use you, but I can't guarantee that a tutor in your field would be needed when you graduate from college. It would be impossible for me now to promise you a job for later. But," he continued, "even if no tutors would be needed, you might consider being a lay reader for an English teacher. Lately, there's been quite a trend toward that sort of thing. Consider it. It would be something you could do from home, and you could work at your own pace."

I thought he was reassuring. If I couldn't teach in a classroom (and he really hadn't even hinted at that), there were two good possibilities for a teacher — tutoring and lay reading. I was sure that was what I needed.

I was wrong. I was turned down and refused any help whatsoever.

"But why?" I managed to ask. "I don't understand." I had come to dread these visits from the counselor with his dismal pessimism. I sensed he did not like me, but he couldn't just refuse to help. He had to have reasons.

"All right, I'll spell it out," he said. "First, anybody as crippled as you can't go to college. No college will accept you, and you can't get a degree if you can't get to college."

"How do you know? What colleges have you tried?"

His eyes narrowed. "I know my field. But ok, say by chance some college *did* accept you. No school system would *ever* hire you."

I shook my head in disbelief. Through tears I said, "I *know* I can teach. All I need is a chance."

He was triumphant. "All right," he said, "suppose by some chance a school system *did* hire you. You couldn't keep the job! How could you teach? How could you control a class? The kids wouldn't respect you."

How could he say that?

Mother cut in, "You can't know that. She deserves the chance to try."

"Oh, no," he said. "I got a trust not to waste the taxpayers' money. Helping her become a teacher would be like pouring water down a rat hole. I can't spend money when I know it won't work out. Now I'll tell you what I can do. I can help set her up in her own business selling magazines from home, or I can get her training to become a proofreader. Either one of those and she'd have a job when she finished."

Mother's tone was icy. "I think you know we are not interested in that. We want her to get her college degree."

"Then I can't help you," he said.

"Would you at least put your reasons for refusing us in writing?"

"No," he told Mother. "You understand what I said."

A door had not just been shut; it had been slammed. I was angry. What kind of counselor would advise someone with a severe visual handicap to become a proofreader?

I remembered the "job" my uncle had arranged for me, selling building products by telephone solicitation for a friend of his while he and the friend went off to the horse races for the afternoon. It was before push button phones, and I could dial only by hooking the index finger of my left hand into the hole while my right arm pulled my hand around the dial. Many times I slipped and had to start over again.

I knew that I was being used. Mother had urged me to quit when she saw how difficult each call was. I was to receive no pay unless a call resulted in an actual sale, and none did. I took my mother's advice and quit. I hated those calls anyway. Nobody knew who I was or that I was crippled, but every time I gave my sales pitch, I felt like a beggar asking for charity.

I felt degraded by the whole episode. Please, not again, God! Being told to sell magazines from home would be the same sort of situation. We had prayed so hard for help and guidance, yet we seemed to be getting nowhere.

Mother recalled a few years earlier when she had been one of the speakers at a meeting at the Palmer House in Chicago. The featured speaker had been Vernon Nickell, the state superintendent of schools. She had heard him say that no child should be denied an education because of a physical handicap. He was still the state superintendent. If only he knew how frustrated I was from trying to get into the University of Illinois. If only. . .

We had a friend who was a state food inspector, and suddenly we wondered if L.D. might know Vernon Nickell. We drove out to L.D.'s farm and explained how the Division of Vocational Rehabilitation had turned me down and that my letters to the university were unanswered. Yes, L.D. had known Vernon Nickell since their college days together and would speak to him at once. L.D. was back to me in a day or two telling me to write again and explain my situation fully, but this time I should send a carbon copy to Vernon Nickell. I did exactly that.

I honestly don't know just what happened. I think that on the day my letters arrived, Vernon Nickell put in a call to the president of the university who instantly got in touch with Professor Timothy J. Nugent, head of the student rehabilitation program. Practically by return mail, I received information on the program and a personal letter. This was in February of 1956, and I accepted the invitation to come to the campus in April for an interview.

"Great is Thy faithfulness! Great is Thy faithfulness!"
Morning by morning new mercies I see!
All I have needed Thy hand hath provided —
"Great is Thy faithfulness," Lord, unto me!

I was instantly impressed with Mr. Nugent. He was filled with energy and obviously excited about the program he had put together at this huge university. He liked the challenges of accommodating a sprawling campus to the needs of physically restricted students, and he was masterful in handling problems. Nevertheless, he was a realist. He told us frankly that the university had never had a student as severely handicapped as I. In the few cases where students had been on campus who needed attendant care, there had been no real success. Student aides had proved unreliable, and living off campus in a nursing home had also been unsatisfactory. However, he did not discourage me in my dream of becoming a teacher. He was a little skeptical about classroom teaching, but if I were only preparing for tutoring, perhaps the student teaching requirement could be waived. He suggested continuing my education by correspondence courses, as only 30 hours of on-campus classes were actually required for graduation. He felt I should get an electric wheelchair and promised to work on a program for me. I left greatly encouraged.

I never really thanked Vernon Nickell except through our friend L.D., but I often wondered if he had known for whom he was speaking. Could Mother's speech have left as much of an impression on him as his had on her? Sometimes I think people at the university wondered just what my connection was.

That summer I gathered a little practical teaching experience. A young man asked me to tutor his wife — an Italian girl who spoke no English. I spoke no Italian, but I wanted to try. With no textbook and only an Italian/English dictionary, I made her daily lessons in English. My best source for her vocabulary lessons was a Montgomery Ward catalog. Earlier I had tutored a young lad in mathematics skills. One summer I taught Sunday school, but the most realistic experience was the year I taught daily vacation Bible school. I had 22 fifth graders in a classroom situation. Since I couldn't push my own wheelchair, I had an older boy as my classroom aide. John Van Arsdale, the husband of a teacher friend of mine who operated his own taxi service, took me back and forth to church each day. Inability to demonstrate the craft projects frustrated me, but all else went well. Yet I knew a regular class would be different — especially with discipline. Even so, I began to see possibilities for regular classroom teaching.

In 1957 my parents and I went to the campus for my second interview. I met Mr. Frank Noble who would serve as my advisor. He and Mr. Nugent planned to have me complete my junior year before I came on campus. I could take a large number of English and social studies courses through correspondence to complete my double major and almost all the educational requirements except student teaching.

Mr. Noble approved my correspondence courses but substituted short story writing and business letter writing for two literature choices. This broadened my English major and didn't weight it as heavily in literature. Although both he and Mr. Nugent agreed summer would be the best time for me to be on campus, student teaching was not offered then. Tentatively, he scheduled me to take the student teaching and methods course during the second semester of 1958—59. He felt the actual teaching experience could be in Elgin as the university did place some student teachers there. I would also take the 1959 summer session on campus which would almost fulfill the residency requirements.

I could take the exam for a provisional teaching certificate (which should be no problem as a college senior) and be ready to teach in the fall of 1959 if there was an opening. I would return to campus for the 1960 summer session to complete my degree and the residency requirements and graduate in August. It looked good to me — a little intense after the pace of college work I'd been doing and a little frightening, but certainly possible. It would be a race to complete a year's work by correspondence due to the limited number of courses that could be taken at one time and the rate at which lessons could be submitted. I would try. My parents agreed.

That day I enrolled in my first correspondence courses and bought books. Soon it was obvious that these would be lengthy, difficult, time-consuming lessons. Some courses forbade submitting a lesson until the previous one had been returned. I began reading carefully and typing page after page. Every single correspondence course I ever took was hard — far harder than class work. I remember when my first lesson in Russian history was returned with the notation that it was too brief. Each lesson was to be at least 20 pages long. I redid it, and the professor sent a note congratulating me. He wrote that most students "threw in the towel" when they discovered the requirements.

I took final exams at our local college with a proctor. No test was easy, and course grades were based largely on the final. Perhaps that was necessary to compensate for the possibility that students had help on the 20 or more regular lessons. Although I typed my finals on Dad's old portable typewriter, my pace was slow. The time limits always caused extra tension. I earned a B on a four-hour geography course because of a poor final. My careful lessons with maps drawn in ink, accurate temperature charts, and A after A had hardly counted. Although I finished every course I ever started, I was always behind in my schedule. Reading, typing, and illustrating lessons were slow processes.

The dean of the college of education approved my program in the summer of 1958. I had completed the two science requirements — one course each semester — at the community college. I made application to be in the student teaching course as planned and again had to approach the local superintendent for permission to do my student teaching in Elgin. He said that would depend on whether a teacher would agree to accept me.

Finding an electric wheelchair required effort. I had tried the chair of a friend and was convinced I could operate one. The day before Thanksgiving 1958 the chair was delivered. After more than nine years of moving only when others moved me, the new freedom was exciting. At first I moved about the house only on low speed, but as I became surer of operating the chair, I used the high speed at all times. High speed was about half the rate of normal walking. Eventually, we joked that the chair had two speeds — slow and slower.

I daily recognized that a faithful God was taking care of me through my wonderful parents — my greatest earthly blessing. Although we had been encouraged to find someone to live with me and care for me, we really didn't try very hard. My mother had offered to come with me again, as she had to Warm Springs. We had applied for a small apartment in the graduate/staff apartments right on campus. This would again leave Dad alone, but he was traveling a great deal for his company and was willing to "batch it" again for my sake. So many details were being worked out for us at the university that we trusted God was using all kinds of people. When Mother offered she would come with me, Mr. Nugent recognized this would be the most reliable roommate I could hope to find, even though he wanted me to face the independence of being on my own. When he expressed concern about the university's liability for one as handicapped as I, my parents waived all right to liability claims should anything happen to me on campus. God would take care of me. We were anxious to remove any reasons that might prevent me from getting "on" campus.

With the electric wheelchair, student teacher applications completed, and correspondence courses continuing, there was nothing to do but wait for official word to come. When Christmas and the New Year came and went without any word, I secretly feared some delay would keep me from that second semester. Then one evening I received a phone call from Mr. Nugent. Everything was ready. We had an apartment, and I was to be on campus the last Friday of January to register. Great is Thy faithfulness! Thank you, God, thank you!

Packing was a challenge. Dad intended to get us down in one

trip in our four-door Buick. In addition to clothes, we needed light housekeeping items — dishes, cooking pots, bedding, iron and ironing board, radio, clock, typewriter, books, etc. The apartment, we were told, was furnished with a sofabed and a table and chairs. In addition we had to take one not-very-portable electric wheelchair with battery and charger and one folding wheelchair. We only needed winter clothes, as we would be home in six weeks for the student teaching. Dad removed the back seat of the car, and with this added space and the large trunk he got everything in. We would all ride in the front seat.

We arrived on campus January 31, 1959, and reported to the rehabilitation center first. We could not go to our apartment to unpack, as it was not yet vacated. Martha, another wheelchair student, had failed courses and was not to be back the second semester. She had gone home during semester break, and the apartment was not yet empty. In the meantime, Jack, a premed student from Chicago, was the volunteer who took me through registration at the Armory. It was a confusing, new situation for me, but not for Jack. I signed where he said and tried to keep track of my growing pile of course cards.

My parents waited at the center as Mr. Nugent tried to clear the apartment for me. When I returned, there was still no clearance. Martha's rent was actually paid through Saturday. Mr. Nugent suggested we either find a motel for the weekend or go home. Non-handicapped students registered the first of the week, and I was not needed on campus before Wednesday. The logical choice seemed to be to make the tiring, three-hour trip home and come back on Tuesday. I had a brief appointment with Mr. Noble, picked up books at the bookstore, unloaded nothing, and left for home in the waning hours of daylight.

We were home again late Saturday night laughing about the shortest college career in history, but also disappointed by the inconsiderate actions of Martha. We were unaware of just how rough she was going to make our lives. We unpacked only the necessities from the car and even went to church on Sunday with our car loaded to the windows. But those bonus days were restless days at home. None of us really wanted to start anything as we felt so temporary. I had completed my correspondence courses and was waiting for the return of several lessons. I would have one final to take later on campus. Dad had appointments on Monday, but we planned to return to Champaign on Tuesday. Martha should be cleared out and well away.

Fortunately, we were simply forging ahead, asking God's help to complete this college education. If we had been praying for a sign, we might have given up much earlier after our trouble in getting a reply from the university or with the reluctance to have me on campus. Now that I was finally accepted, my housing hadn't been ready. Little did I realize that even worse obstacles lay ahead. The weather reports gave the first hint. A major winter storm was headed across the state.

None of us slept well that night. We awoke even earlier than the early alarm to find a blizzard raging outside. Should we even start out? Dad made the decision since he was the driver. We would start; we could always turn back if conditions became too difficult or put up in a motel somewhere. Once again the last items were loaded into the car. We left well before seven for what should have been a three-hour drive. Visibility was extremely poor, and blowing snow reduced it even more as we reached the open highway. Dad's hope was that since we were driving south, we might drive out of it. The miles seemed endless with speed at less than 20 miles an hour in some places. Not wanting to distract the driver, we sat in stony silence, all eyes straining through the swirling snow. I suggested once that we could turn back, but Dad was grimly determined to press on. He said we'd make it if it grew no worse. Prayer was our constant companion.

Somewhere, sometime, we passed the halfway point and continued on. Needless to say, there was little other traffic. The snow began to change to sleet and freezing rain, and we heard new sounds of slivers of ice hitting the windshield. Dad had always been a good driver and kept his cars in top condition. We were warm, had plenty of gas, and certainly had the weight to hold the car on the road. We kept on. Just after noon we arrived on campus and headed for the tar-paper barracks section where the rehabilitation center was. Mr. Nugent was out, and Dad could get no information on our apartment, so we waited in the car. We were hungry but didn't know where the nearest eating place was, and we didn't want to risk missing Mr. Nugent. Weeks later we would find out that half a block away in another barracks structure was a diner where we could have eaten. Instead we waited.

At three o'clock Mr. Nugent returned. The news for us was not good. Martha hadn't vacated her apartment, and her father was using his connections to fight her expulsion. We were not going to have an apartment after all. Late in the afternoon, after numerous calls to housing, Mr. Nugent offered us the best he could — a furnished sleeping room in a different building with a good chance for another apartment in 10 days to two weeks. We had no choice but to take it, but darkness was already setting in as the sleet continued. We weren't even unpacked.

Mr. Nugent sent a man over to help and show Dad where to back down a driveway to the basement entrance of our building. We parked a few feet from the door. Dad put me in the wheelchair first; I stayed just inside the basement door. Mother went up with Dad with the first load and stayed in the room as Wally and Dad made trips back and forth until everything was upstairs.

It was just about six o'clock when we finally had everything upstairs and crowded into the room. No one had had anything to eat since our predawn breakfast. The strain and fatigue were getting to us all. We called for a carry-out supper and had it delivered. As we ate, we took stock of our situation. The room was furnished with a three-quarter size sofabed, a lounge chair, a desk and chair, and a small chest of drawers — all in nice condition. There was a closet and private bath. Now there were also suitcases, cartons of household items, two wheelchairs, a pile of school books, and three adults. It was crowded, but warm and snug.

Dad's original plans were to make a turn-around trip, but the weather and our late schedule made that impossible. We really had no place for him to stay, as Mother and I would have to share the sofabed. However, he laid the sofa cushions on the floor along the wall and added the cushion from the lounge chair to improvise himself a bed. We were glad to have his company as he was good at working out problems, and it looked like there could be many. I was tired and discouraged enough to want to go home, but there was no turning back.

The sleet had stopped by morning, but everything was a sheet of ice. Dad and Mother had gotten a few groceries the night before. She made us breakfast on the desk. With an electric coffee pot, toaster, and frying pan plus a natural ice box on the oustide window sill, we had the rudiments of a kitchen. Dad left for home by nine, and Mother began to organize the room. The sofabed had to be made up first just to have space in the room. There were laundry facilities in the basement plus storage space for the suitcases. It was a fine temporary solution.

In the afternoon I ventured out to get the bus with the hydraulic lift to go to the rehabilitation center. I found the icy sidewalks too difficult for the electric wheelchair and blew five fuses in an hour. Fortunately, Mother was with me to release the motors and push the heavy chair by hand. Mr. Nugent was glad we were adapting and not making trouble for him. I hoped he wasn't worried that Vernon Nickell might be on my case again.

After telling me the bus would pick me up at 7:30 next morning for my first class, Mr. Nugent sent us by bus to the Durst Cycle Shop to have my fuse problem checked. Mr. Durst, who was a genius with wheelchairs, quickly discovered that I had only 15-amp fuses and needed 30s. He also made several repairs and corrections on my "new" chair. We returned to our building at twilight. Inch-thick ice was everywhere, and I blew another fuse. Getting around would not be easy — even with bigger fuses.

Mother and I were both awake before the alarm for my first day of classes. We left our building by 7:20. It took us only three minutes, but I was glad to be early and not risk missing the bus. We took turns waiting — one always out on the curbing while the other was behind a corner of a building a little out of the sharp wind. The bitter cold deepened. We didn't dare go back up the long sidewalk and around the corner to the vestibule of our building for fear of missing the bus. At 7:55 it arrived — loaded with both boys and girls as the boys' driver hadn't shown up. I was the last one on and had to get off to let others out at the first several stops. Once we got to Gregory Hall, Mother pushed the chair because of the ice and our lateness, but I was still 15 minutes tardy.

There was no way to maneuver on my own with all the ice, so Mother waited to push me to my Lincoln Hall class. That professor didn't show up, so it was back to Gregory Hall for the methods class. By noon we were back to the bus for a roundabout ride home.

How good to open the sofa, lie down, cover up, get warm, and review the morning! One thing was clear: The power chair could not be used until the ice melted.

On Friday we tried Plan B. The power wheelchair was shelved. Instead, Mother pushed me in the hand chair for a 7:15 pickup on the boys' bus. We rode the route and were let out at Gregory Hall at 7:40 in plenty of time for the 8:00 class. Mother brought a book along to spend her morning waiting to push me to my Lincoln Hall class and back. I hated the idea, but there was no alternative until the ice melted enough for me to use the power chair.

When Mother appeared after class, three young women from my class volunteered to get me back and forth each day and out to the bus at noon. Carolyn, the engineer of the operation, was experienced with wheelchairs as her grandmother had used one for 20 years. Jerry and Diane were equally willing to offer Plan C. All Mother would have to do was meet the bus at noon. She could wait inside the foyer of a building up a few steps and watch for the bus.

By the time I was home for lunch, I could see things would work out. If I could take notes fast enough, keep up with the reading, and get papers typed, I should be able to make it. The ice had to melt eventually, and we were scheduled to get our apartment in 10 days. I felt sure God was taking care of us.

Earlier, when my picture had appeared in the paper receiving my electric wheelchair, I received a phone call from a woman who had been my fellow student in night classes. She introduced me by phone to her daughter Sherry who was a student at the university. Sherry pledged to check on us when we arrived on campus and offered to help us any way she could. True to her word, she and another Elgin-area girl were our first visitors that weekend. Their gift of a live plant made us feel welcomed. Other than that, it was a quiet, hopeful weekend. Mother attended church across the street; the many steps and the ice kept me away.

By Monday the school routine seemed established. That afternoon it began to rain, melting some of the treacherous ice, but our weather problems were not over. I'm not sure if the winter of 1959 set any records for central Illinois, but it was certainly a hard one. Rain was followed by sleet, ice, and snow in repeating cycles. I, who had only gone out in winter when Dad took me by car, found myself trying to be independent in a power wheelchair on a vast, sprawling campus. Many days I used this chair over Mother's objections, preferring the independence and mobility in class regardless of the risk of blown fuses. At times I sat on patches of ice spinning my wheels, but never for long. The campus was filled with good Samaritans who simply saw the need and moved in with the necessary push or pull.

Mother also worried about my health since I was out in the weather so much. Colds were a real threat as they could lead to respiratory difficulties, and my breathing was delicate. My severe asthma attack had added another problem to my history of hayfever and allergies complicated by my polio weakness. Cold air was difficult to breathe, and I sometimes found myself gasping on the bitter cold mornings. I tried to dismiss the threat, but it was a genuine concern to Mother.

"What will you do when it rains?" she asked.

"I'll get wet," I answered.

"Don't be flip," she cautioned. "This is not funny. It takes you a long time to get to classes from the bus. You could get awfully wet. And if you catch cold, I'm the one that has to take care of you."

She was most concerned about a lapful of rain and sitting all morning in damp clothes. When I asked other wheelchair students' advice, the common solution seemed to be a plastic cleaner bag across the lap and books that could be tucked in along each side of the wheelchair next to the arms. I thought that sounded adequate, but Mother was not convinced. One day she arrived home from the grocery store with a full length plastic raincoat. She thought she had solved the problem.

"But Mother," I countered, "it's a full length coat. It won't fit me." I never wore long coats, as I couldn't raise myself to let a long coat slide down over my hips. I wore only short coats and jackets.

"You can wear it backwards," she said.

"How will that look?"

"It doesn't matter how it looks if it keeps you well. You know what your father would say."

Indeed I did. He always despaired over my vanity. I was always willing to suffer considerable discomfort if doing so improved appearances. However, I hadn't conceded the raincoat battle yet. "If

88

I'm supposed to wear it backwards, why did you buy me a coat with a hood?"

No argument stopped Mother. "That's all they had."

I gave up ungraciously, muttering that I'd look like a horse with a feed bag on. There was always the outside chance that it would only rain nights or weekends when I could stay inside.

My health really was an unknown factor. This experience marked my first attempt at attending classes full-time since polio. Although I had all my classes in the morning, I also had therapy two afternoons a week, trips to the library, beauty shop appointments, and church. This could be taxing. Away from our family and friends, we expected almost no social life, but this proved incorrect. Friends and relatives came down on weekends, and it was no trouble at all to find classmates and fellow wheelchair students who would come for Mother's home-cooked meals. Eventually, we had to restrict involvement. Getting the education was the first priority.

We received word we could move into an apartment February 13. With help from the rehab center, we were sure we could move ourselves upstairs to #627, but Dad said he would be down on Valentine's Day. He brought us a floor lamp and my last correspondence lessons, which had arrived at home. I would take the final on campus at the center. Our new apartment seemed spacious and empty, though in reality it was only one large room with sofabed and drop-leaf table with four chairs, a small kitchen, and bathroom. A built-in cupboard had a middle section of shelves and drawers that could be left open like a bookcase. On Dad's next trip, he borrowed Aunt Vange's station wagon and brought down a lounge chair for Mother, a study lamp to use on the table, and some folding trays to use as end tables. We bought an extra bookcase. The only problem was that I did not sleep well on the soft sofabed, and it was too low for Mother to help me. Mr. Nugent ordered a single bed for me from housing, one usually set up for emergency housing only. It was higher and much better, but it had an even softer, lumpy mattress. Our building superintendent, who had come to know Mother and her homemade cookies for his daily coffee break, came to our rescue. He fastened an old closet door to the bed frame to make it firm and obtained a new firm mattress from somewhere. From then on it was ideal.

I was not surprised to find that therapy was required by the state to fulfill the physical education requirement for graduation. For those able to participate, it included swimming and driver's education in specially equipped cars. I was involved only in the therapy. As at the local hospital where I first had polio, I was the most severely involved and could participate only on a limited basis. I knew my therapist was a joker the first day I met him. Although Mother had followed an exercise program with me on a daily basis when I first returned from

Warm Springs, those exercises gradually became less regular as my days became too busy. I had not been stretched for some time — especially by a no-nonsense, professional therapist like Mr. Elmer. He gave me a strenuous workout that first day. I pleaded for mercy only half in jest, telling him he should take it easy on my first day.

"That's what I *am* doing," he replied. My feet and legs ached for hours after his "easy" routine. I was dismayed to realize I was to get a grade in therapy.

"What do I have to do to get an *A?*" I asked.

Mr. Elmer had a quick answer. "You have to give your therapist a Valentine and bring him homemade cookies every week." I'm not sure if he knew at that point that I was on campus with my mother. As I mentally considered getting a headache every therapy afternoon, I was already plotting my own survival. I drew a charming (or so I thought) skunk on a card and inscribed it, "Stay as sweet as you are!" and surrounded it with little red hearts — Part I of my campaign! Mother took over the rest and made the therapy gang a box of cookies every week — chocolate chip, spice, raisin, chocolate, etc. Mr. Elmer said he wasn't sure about me, but Mother definitely got an *A!*

My studies became even more of a joy than the rowdy fun of therapy. All of my classes were composed of the same students, most in their last semester of college preparing to be secondary English teachers in the fall. We were getting at the nitty-gritty of teaching — practicing lessons on our classmates, preparing units to take with us student teaching, and previewing loads of new materials. The two teachers, J. N. Hook and F. James Rybak, were fantastic. They instilled professionalism. We all joined the National Council of Teachers of English, which Dr. Hook headed. They told us we would all owe a debt to our cooperating teachers that we would repay by training at least one student teacher each during our careers.

Both men became students when we all practiced teaching in front of the group. Quite often "little Jimmy Hook" was the bad boy in class who quickly pinpointed weaknesses in our lesson plans. The comments of these two dedicated teachers on my individual lessons encouraged me greatly. If they ever felt I couldn't teach in a regular classroom, they never indicated a single doubt or concern to me. I felt they believed in me.

I looked forward to student teaching with both anxiety and expectation. Most of my classmates would be teaching in the Champaign-Urbana area, but I requested Elgin. I was anxious to prove myself in the system where I hoped to teach. This request meant some changes at the university. Because no other English teachers would be in that area, it would be costly to send a supervisor 300 miles round trip to check on one teacher. Since several social studies teachers were to be in that area, their supervisor was assigned an extra teacher—me. He accepted. It was another of several accommodations that huge university (an institution usually considered to be impersonal) willingly made for me, an individual student. Mr. Thompson had found a junior high school teacher willing to take a student teacher in a wheelchair. I had already corresponded with her and found out a little of what her classes would be studying when I came. In preparation I had already read *Ivanhoe.*

We kept our apartment but left keys with the neighbors. We took home only our winter clothes, typewriter, books, and wheelchairs. How good home looked! We felt things were working so smoothly that God had to be watching over us. We were home Saturday night, March 21, and I was expected to be at Larsen Junior High School Monday morning. I packed my little briefcase with everything but my lunch on Sunday and reviewed my paperback of *Ivanhoe.*

Rose Reber was something else, a career teacher who knew her subject well. She was every inch a professional—always smartly groomed as if coming each day to teach young people was very important to her. She was always prepared, always on time, and always in control. I didn't fully appreciate at the time what a sacrifice it was for her to take me. She was teaching six classes a day—three English and three reading—in an overcrowded school while a new school was under construction. On what should have been her plan period, she had lunch duty—the only part of her schedule that I never assumed. When I came in late March, her classes were beautifully under control and very respectful.

I kept the electric wheelchair at school in a janitor's closet, and John Van Arsdale took me back and forth each day in his cab. I had a table/desk in Mrs. Reber's conference room. Her classroom was already full with the overcrowded classes. I carried a sack lunch and ate each day at the library table at the back of her room.

It had been 10 years since I had been in a regular public school classroom, and I still loved it all. I sat at the back of the room with the seating charts, learning students' names and observing the general routines. I was mentally adapting procedures to fit my limitations. I could have a student put the absence slip in the high clip outside the door. Students would do any blackboard writing. I felt I could handle it all with careful preplanning.

Gradually, I began to teach—first one class and then all three sections of that subject. Mrs. Reber observed. Later, in our after-school conference time, she questioned my techniques, made me justify what I had chosen to emphasize, checked to see if I had noted various classroom occurrences, impressed on me how many threads a teacher must handle at all times, and made me learn.

I worried about my handwriting. I could and did type ditto

masters and lesson plans at home. I checked short answer tests and quizzes. These were no problem, but would students who were used to Mrs. Reber's flowing Palmer script be able to read my shaky comments on their papers? I offered to decipher and translate all unreadable parts, but they accepted my uneven scrawl without complaint. I should have had more faith in them. I had noticed that as Mrs. Reber put me more and more on my own and began to leave the room, they didn't fall apart. Hardly anyone acted up. They were so good for me — as if they wanted to help me succeed. They probably never suspected their impact on me. Without any words they were telling me I could teach.

Quickly the days sped, and Friday, May 8, approached. I had learned so much those weeks. I could never adequately thank Mrs. Reber. After all, accepting a student teacher in a wheelchair was far different than accepting an able-bodied one.

I was back in classes again at the university on May 11. We were all eager to share our frontline experiences. We were like troops reunited, and were not without our casualties. One had dropped out completely, recognizing that teaching was not for him. Some had felt their cooperatng teachers had been totally incompetent; others hated theirs. How lucky I had been! A few had been so successful that they already had jobs for the fall. I had taken the exam for a provisional teaching certificate, since I would be only six hours short of my degree by the end of summer. I had also applied for a teaching position in the new junior high less than a mile from my home that would be partially opened that fall. I would also be willing to be a substitute. My application letter was never answered, a shadow of things to come.

I had to see my student teaching supervisor once more for my final evaluation based on his observations and Mrs. Reber's comments. My appointment was just before therapy one afternoon, and I was concerned about having to go for the interview in slacks. In those days, skirts and dresses were the normal fashion for college girls — at least, for classes and appointments like this. I decided I would explain my outfit just briefly as we began.

I waited for the bus, tense with expectancy and a tinge of dread. So much hung on success in student teaching. I wished for the bus to be early, but it was late. However, the driver was so joyous that I could not complain. He had just become a father. As I congratulated him, he slipped a cigar in my shirt pocket over my protests that I didn't smoke. I hurried up the sidewalk to Greg Hall hoping the outside door would be open to the warm day — which it was — and that the elevator wouldn't be tied up — which it wasn't. I arrived just on time, and Professor Hahn was waiting for me.

He told me good things about my student teaching experience. When people compliment me, my mind has a way of going blank. I suspect I just sat there and smiled. Then he handed me a lightly sealed envelope.

"It's your grade," he said.

I opened it as smoothly as I could and extracted a white card. On it was the single letter A. "Oh, thank you," I said, audibly to him and to God in my heart. "This is like getting an Oscar," I added, and then I looked down at myself. I had forgotten to mention why I was wearing slacks, and protruding from my pocket was a cigar! I quickly explained my clothes and the gift cigar.

"I was wondering if you had a few bad habits I hadn't noticed," he said, his eyes twinkling.

"Do you smoke?" I asked.

"An occasional cigar," he replied. The solution was obvious.

The May days sped past. It was good to be back on campus and feel familiar this time. As before, I caught a cold and suffered with a sore throat and laryngitis. This was the beginning of a pattern of weakness that would establish itself in me, sometimes followed by lingering coughs. I missed classes on only one day, but I felt weak and limp for some time. In addition, we seemed to have a lot of company. Mother seemed to have something freshly baked each day when I returned, and everything disappeared. Our dear neighbors Stephanie and Julie often stopped by in the evening just about the time I finished studying and needed a break. Many wheelchair friends came. Sometimes we visited with Betty Arnett and her three children. Brock, her oldest, was big enough to come up alone on the elevator and visit us. One day he arrived with fresh, warm pieces of pineapple upside-down cake. His visits were a special treasure, as we missed our favorite neighborhood children. We found such good people everywhere at the university (Martha had been the exception), and we forged some lasting friendships.

We returned home for the few weeks before the summer session began, and then it was back to campus with a window air conditioner. Summer school seemed rather anticlimactic after the excitement of student teaching, but one professor in my writing course truly challenged me that summer. I despaired during Dr. Hogan's classes, but I was learning the disciplines necessary to be a writer and the writer's obligation to honesty. By example, he also taught me that a good teacher works much harder than his students. Because of him, I believe that writing can be taught—a position that has helped me believe in my own students' abilities and their capacities to improve.

Prairie summers are hot, and 1959 was no exception. No building where I had any class was air conditioned, but when I returned home, our little apartment was a cool oasis. It became popular with friends in the building who had no air conditioning, and we had lots of company. Every Monday night Mother and I previewed the educational films shown on campus. She would push me over to the auditorium in my hand chair, as the bus did not run at night. She pushed me also to the health center for my weekly allergy shot and to the beauty shop. We watched the Fourth of July parade from our apartment lawn, which was right on the parade route. That night a special bus took us to the stadium for the fireworks display. We entertained a lot—neighbors, fellow students, the bus driver, friends and relatives from home—though sometimes just for quick lunches, then back to studying. Almost every other weekend Dad came. The summer schedule was different. Papers assigned one day were often due the next. I kept up, but sometimes only with great effort. How quickly time passed!

In July I was invited to membership in Kappa Delta Pi, a national honor society in education. My first reaction was to skip the honor, but Mother insisted I consult Mr. Nugent. He told me to join. First, he said, honors coming to handicapped students made the whole program look good. Second, it would help on any job application if I could list honor society membership. I hadn't thought about that.

My application to teach in Elgin was being totally ignored. Lacking only six hours for my degree and with a provisional certificate, I was hoping to teach and then return to campus in the summer of 1960 to finish both the degree and residency requirements. By the end of July I realized I was not going to be hired. I don't even think I was disappointed. I knew how exhausted I was. I could not be as ready as I would want to be by the end of August.

Not getting a job and my good grades at the university made possible a change in plans. Through Mr. Nugent's office, I petitioned the university to waive residency requirements. That would allow me to take one course by correspondence and one offered by extension at the Elgin Community College, and I would complete my degree back home. I could do this easily with spare time to tutor or do substitute teaching if opportunities arose. It was a good plan, but would such a big school make such a concession? It would and did. Once again the marvelous University of Illinois met my individual needs.

When the end was in sight, and I knew I would finish my degree, I thought about the State Division of Vocational Rehabilitation. What a shame it hadn't taken a chance on me! I doubt if any program could have cost less. Our apartment from February through August was $70 a month. We purchased electricity from the university power plant, usually less than two dollars a month. Tuition was $100 for the semester, including student teaching, and $50 for summer school. I always sold my books back. Besides, we hadn't even asked for financial help—just for help in being admitted. Obviously, we didn't need it. Our help came from the Lord. I had often heard that He has no hands but our hands. I could never thank those countless helping hands that had reached out to us, but God knew whose they were. I prayed He would bless them all—most especially my precious parents.

Dad came down the first weekend in August and took home the first load of things. As I crammed for finals, Mother paid bills, sold my books, packed our possessions, followed university procedures for vacating, and generally prepared to terminate our stay so inauspiciously begun seven months earlier. When Dad returned a week later, we were ready. With his engineering skills, he maneuvered the air conditioner, wheelchair, and our assorted belongings into the car quickly and smoothly. We turned in our keys and left for home that afternoon.

Finishing my degree was easy. The two courses comprised my lightest load ever in college and were finished in early 1960. Though I had time, I was never once called to either tutor or substitute.

Through the rehabilitation program I had placed an order for a used IBM electric typewriter whenever one became available. Because I was handicapped, I was eligible to purchase one for just the trade-in allowance. IBM reconditioned each machine free. In January at semester break our friend Bill brought my typewriter from Champaign. After the years of taxing my limited strength on Dad's old portable, I had my own electric. It would be great to type stencils for school if I was hired to teach.

In March I applied again in Elgin. The first of May I had an interview at my home with both the suprintendent and his assistant. They were not encouraging. Although the new junior high would open fully that fall, they didn't know at that time what openings there would be.

I waited. I had come so far that I couldn't believe I would be denied the chance to teach somewhere. What had seemed such an impossible dream during high school had become a reality. I lived on the hope that, just as there had been a college for me, there would also be a classroom.

> Pardon for sin and a peace that endureth,
> Thy own dear presence to cheer and to guide,
> Strength for today and bright hope for tomorrow,
> Blessings all mine, with ten thousand beside!

> "Great is Thy faithfulness!"

I knew from experience that my plans were not always the same as God's. I thought I was aiming toward a career of useful service in an honorable profession, but was that enough? During my college years Dad's dreams for his professional future had crumbled to dust around him.

Dad had joined Bill in the engineering firm they expected to own someday where they worked together so well. For Dad it was a little like having a son again, as Bill was a much younger man. They were in no hurry to have the current owners retire; just knowing that they would someday was enough to dream about and plan for. Money would not be a hurdle, as Bill was an only child who had inherited farms. There seemed to be no problem.

As Bill and his wife awaited the birth of their second child, he mentioned his concern for his own health. He felt heavy, tight in his chest, and had difficulty breathing, he said, but passed it off as the result of being a little overweight. As soon as the baby was born, he promised Dad he'd consult a doctor about himself. But Bill's discomfort grew, and he reluctantly entered a hospital for tests. He died on the operating table during exploratory surgery. He was filled with undetected cancer. Two weeks later his second son was born.

Once again our world reeled. Although Mother and I had not known Bill as long or as well as Dad, we had come to love the family. We also knew how much it meant to Dad to work with Bill and plan their future. The Bible has told us that we know not what a day may bring (Prov. 27:1). The joy of one day turned to the sorrow of the next; the hope of one to the despair of another. Again, it was God who sent His unfailing comfort and renewed our hopes.

Of course, Dad continued working in the firm. When it was time to buy the business, money was a concern. There was no way Dad could raise enough to buy the whole company even though the purchase terms were good. What finally evolved was that Dad bought 40 percent, the man who replaced Bill bought 40 percent, and another employee bought the remaining 20. It was a far-from-perfect partnership with too many differing ideas for running the business. Perhaps nothing would have been as satisfactory for Dad as the dream he had shared with Bill.

Even in disappointment there are blessings. When Dad had to take his physical for partnership insurance, his condition as a potential diabetic was discovered. Since diabetes had been a contributing factor in Grandmother Bramer's death, we felt the guidance of God in this early warning for Dad. Immediately, he began losing the 40 pounds the doctor recommended and stopped using sugar completely. For years his condition was controlled by diet alone.

I wondered what future God had for me — what I hoped for, or, as with Dad's dream, something far different. It was hard waiting those spring days when my college work was completed, but my employment was still unknown.

I was graduated from the University of Illinois on June 18, 1960, at ceremonies I did not attend. I had earned my B.S. degree and qualified for university honors with my grade point average. These were withheld, however, because too many credits were earned through correspondence courses. I would never quibble about that. All I had ever wanted from the university, I had received —the chance to earn a degree. Graduation honors didn't even matter. What did matter was getting a job.

How Great Thou Art

People who knew I would be graduating in June would ask, "What are your plans after graduation?"

My answer was always the same, "I hope to teach." Most wished me good luck; a few seemed skeptical. May passed to June, June to July. Although there was still a teacher shortage, I had heard nothing since my earlier interview. My follow-up phone calls were never returned.

At an Easter Seal board meeting my attorney friend, Frank Kramer, asked about my job status. I gave him my stock reply, but expanded on my situation more under his questioning. Another board member encouraged me to apply at the Catholic high school and offered to be a reference for me. Everyone on the board encouraged me not to give up. I appreciated their support and wished they were all on the school board.

A few days later our phone rang, and a secretary set up an interview at home with the superintendent and assistant superintendent. I was overjoyed; they had to be coming to offer me a contract. My hopes were quickly dashed when they arrived. They were less cordial than previously; in fact, they were nearly hostile. The assistant superintendent began the attack.

"What's the idea of hiring an attorney to get a job?" he demanded.

I was stunned. "What attorney?"

"Franklin Kramer," he sneered as if I was playing coy.

"I did not hire him," I replied. "I don't know what you're talking about." Bit by bit I pieced together the story. Frank had apparently made an appointment to see them and demanded to know why they were ignoring me and for what reasons they were denying me a job. I don't know what was said and probably never will, but I do know

Frank was always a fighter and a champion of basic rights. He could be very persuasive.

"I have never seen anything so unprofessional as to hire a lawyer to get a job," Mr. Walden sputtered.

I pleaded my innocence of any knowledge of the affair. "I did not employ him and will not pay him a cent," I assured them. "In fact, I'm sure he would not even accept a fee if I offered him one." I was deeply hurt. Mr. Thompson had encouraged me to get my education, making me feel I could be useful somewhere. Mr. Walden knew me as his student in his curriculum class just the year before. Yet they treated me as the enemy. I explained what had happened at the Easter Seal meeting which must have led to Attorney Kramer's actions. I tried subtly to suggest the fault was partially their own for ignoring my letter and phone inquiries.

It must have been hard to upbraid me for an attack I hadn't made, for the tone shifted slightly. They began to grill me on what they obviously considered just reasons for not hiring me.

"How will you maintain discipline?" he asked.

"By reason and fairness," I said. "Even teachers physically able to punish aren't supposed to use physical punishment." They knew that.

Mr. Walden pressed on. "What will you do in an emergency?"

"Meet it. Who can guarantee performance in a time of emergency?" I mentioned the Our Lady of Angels School fire in Chicago in 1958, in which many children lost their lives. To my knowledge there wasn't a handicapped person on the staff, yet some nuns were credited with saving lives and others with costing lives. No one could predict his reaction under stress.

"What will you do for your personal needs during the day?"

I promised them I would not need personal help from any staff member or student. For the routine classroom tasks, like moving a set of books, I would enlist student help just as many able-bodied teachers did.

I had been thinking of solutions for potential problems ever since I began preparing to teach, but God was giving me answers that day. I was far from calm because I suspected my whole future was hanging in the balance. My composure was pretty shaky. I was afraid they'd ask about that, too.

But Mother was with me, supporting me on every question. She finally felt they were putting me through too much and asked, "Does every teacher you hire have to answer all these questions?"

They let up somewhat. Maybe it was fear of Attorney Kramer lurking in the background, ready to come to my defense. Perhaps it was Mr. Thompson (who really was a gentleman) simply stopping the inquisition out of a sense of fairness. My memories are too mixed with my emotions to be sure just what happened. I suspect they had agreed before they came on what they were going to do because they did not confer privately before Mr. Walden began summing up their position.

"Our first responsbility," he said, "is for the welfare of our students." I made no answer. I agreed with that myself. He continued, "We are supported with taxpayers' money. We are not running a charity that can provide a job for every handicapped person who asks for one." Was I that run-of-the-mill? I wondered. I was a local person, the product of their own school system, a college graduate with a good academic record, and a successful student teacher in one of their schools. Could they see nothing beyond the wheelchair? "However," he continued, "we would be willing to risk having you in a regular classroom on a half-time basis." The implication seemed to be that I couldn't do too much harm in half a day. "Would you accept that?"

"Yes." It was not what I wanted, of course, but it was a start. I was sure I could prove myself if only given the chance. This was, at least, a chance.

I was emotionally wrung out when they left, but I had the verbal promise of a job. Mother, always quick to see some benefit in every disappointment, said, "Maybe this is all for the best. After all, we don't know how your strength will hold out."

On July 21, 1960, I signed my first teaching contract for half-time teaching at half of the annual starting salary of $4,700. I honestly think that if I had been asked to pay for the privilege of teaching instead of receiving $2,350, I would have found the money somewhere. My assignment was at the new junior high near my home with one class of eighth-grade English and two of eighth-grade reading. My former mathematics teacher would be my principal, and the assistant principal was a man from our church. Both men remembered me as a junior high student before polio.

John Van Arsdale, my dear taxi man, agreed to take me as a regular customer each school day. Because the electric wheelchair did not collapse easily and would have been a nuisance to transport each day, I needed a second electric wheelchair to leave at school. John would attach it to the charger each night and lock it away in a little closet under the stairs near a back door. Since I would be leading a more active life, I needed a power chair to use at home also. Though the first one had been purchased for me, I exercised my new independence to buy my own—a superior American wheelchair that served me well for more than 20 years.

As soon as my job was official, my parents and I went one summer afternoon to tour the new school. I had a first floor classroom. Everything was wonderfully convenient. There was a freight elevator for those times when I would need to go upstairs or down. The cafeteria was in the basement, but since I would be through at noon,

I would be eating lunch at home. I picked up textbooks and a box of stencils to type at home. Mr. Hulmes, the principal, was still writing students' schedules.

"How's it going?" I asked.

"Well, pretty good," he said. "I could use one more study hall. Some of them are getting pretty big."

"Couldn't I stay later every day and have a study hall?" I volunteered.

His eyes lit up. Clearly he hadn't thought of that option. Then his expression changed. "No, I can't do that. You're only hired for half time. That's only three classes. It would change your status . . ."

I interrupted him. "I don't mean for extra pay. Just let me have a study hall for the experience. Who cares exactly how many periods a day I'm actually at the school?"

He agreed to think about it, and that's the way it worked out. There was no change in status nor pay, but I handled three classes and one supervisory period — two classes less than full time. It was good for me to handle a nonclass situation where students didn't behave out of fear of having grades lowered for misbehavior.

By the time school started, I had my year's work nearly ready. I had made myself large resource notebooks. Tests, exercises, worksheets, and assignment sheets were all typed on stencils. I had collected supplementary materials for every unit. I didn't want anyone to fault me on being poorly prepared.

Those first days are lost in a haze of euphoria. I don't know how everything worked out, but I do know there were no problems. It was amazing how well a physically disabled person with more than 20 willing students in each class could accomplish things. I had resources ready plus very organized plans to minimize any help I would need. From the beginning the students seemed to overlook my handicap and ignore the wheelchair as if neither were there. I had seven of the eight children from my neighborhood in classes that first year. Since they all more or less knew me, they may have spread the word that I wasn't really very unusual. At any rate, my students reacted as if they'd been having wheelchair teachers for every year of school. I felt completely accepted. Praise the Lord!

I worked very hard that year to have good lessons every day. I wanted no student or parent to feel cheated because the teacher was handicapped. The students responded beautifully. I taught nearly the whole period every period, as I had free afternoons at home to grade papers. The half-day schedule actually worked very well for me because it kept me from getting overtired.

One day my principal appeared at my doorway just before reading class and announced he was going to visit that period. We were finishing a story about a blind girl who learned to use a seeing eye dog. *Braille* was one of our vocabulary words, and although most knew what Braille was, few had ever actually seen any. That previous summer I had sent for 35 sample Braille alphabets with a quotation to translate. I passed these out, and everyone, including Mr. Hulmes, tried to read with fingertips. The kids were super-enthusiastic and compassionate in their comments as they discussed their feelings about being blind. I read them excerpts from a book about the first Seeing Eye dog ever used in this country. The period passed quickly, but Mr. Hulmes stayed a minute after the bell rang to congratulate me on both my lesson and my classroom management. The visit, he said, had been his official evaluation, required before I would be considered for a contract next year. Had I realized that, I would have been more nervous. He assured me he would give me a high rating in every category. I felt good.

I volunteered for every committee and every extra assignment. I willingly pushed myself to be the best teacher I could be. I had told myself before I began that my allegiance was to the school board that hired me and the staff where I worked. I would not break rules to win points with students nor be easy on them so they would like me. In fact, I told myself (before I met them) that I didn't even care if they liked me or not; that wasn't important. But as soon as I met them, I knew I wanted their respect and affection. What great students they were! Often since then, when I've had a really good teaching unit, I've wished that I could teach those first-year students again. I could have given them so much more, and they deserved the best.

I organized an English unit called "So Proudly We Hail," in which students read a biography about an outstanding living American. They gave oral book reports to the class so we'd all know the people. Later each wrote a personal letter to one of the famous Americans asking for an autograph for the school collection. The industrial arts department printed autograph cards for us. On the side blackboard (which I didn't use) I mounted a collage-type map of the United States. Against this were pictures of many of the famous people and quotations by them. As the mail came in, the little signed cards were added to the display. What joy to put up signatures of Grandma Moses, John F. Kennedy, Helen Keller, Jackie Robinson, and others! I think our biggest moment came when an embossed envelope (instead of our own self-addressed return envelope) arrived. In it on heavy stationery was a personal letter from Herbert Hoover to the girl who had written him.

Beryl, my taxi man's wife, came into my room one morning and noted the display. When she heard about the unit, she went to the office to drag in Mr. Hulmes who hadn't been there since his class visit. They both studied the autographs, reading list, letters, and pictures. Later that day as I was waiting in the back hall for my taxi, Mr. Hulmes came from his office to talk to me.

"You know," he said, "I think I only made one bad mistake this year."

I picked up my cue. "What was that?"

"I only hired Mary Bramer for half a day. Will you teach full-time for me next year?"

Would I? Definitely! He said some complimentary things, but I hastened to assure him the half day was not a mistake. I didn't regret it. Having to get out so another teacher could use the room forced me to go home and rest. It had been a wise decision all along, even though I had resented it at first.

I finished that first year of teaching without a day's absence. My mother worried that such sustained sitting might cause the fragile skin of the pressure sore to break open, but it didn't. What did wear out were my ears. I was not used to wearing earrings each day as I did when teaching, and the clips caused sores. I had to abandon that part of my finery.

Eventually, however, the long days when I became a full-time teacher took their toll. Sitting in the same chair from about 7:40 A.M. to 4:30 P.M. without being able to stand for a while, switch seats, or even change my position during the day caused the tissue-thin skin across the bone finally to break open. The doctor recommended painting the area with compound tincture of benzoine to toughen the skin. Mother generously painted the whole area, which was about the size of a coaster, with the blackish fluid. Unfortunately, my skin was allergic to this, and the entire area broke out in blisters. These filled with fluid, broke open, and drained to make an ugly, weeping sore. Sitting became almost unbearable, but I wanted to stick it out the few teaching days until Easter vacation.

I always hated to miss school—even as a kid. I wouldn't have minded being absent due to a cold or laryngitis because normal teachers had these problems, too, but I didn't want to miss work because of a problem related to my handicap—like a pressure sore, for example. Reluctantly, Mother let me try. She folded a pad of muslin sheeting to a thickness of 32 layers and tied and taped it over the sore. Dad bought foam rubber and cut a seat cushion with a hole in it to accommodate the sore area. I took aspirin to fight the pain. It was not comfortable, but I endured, although the bandage pad would be soaked through by the time I got home each day.

I had only slight hopes of getting the sore healed over vacation. It was too tender and raw, but my faith was too small. A nurse friend told us that her favorite remedy for bed sores was a coating of raw egg white painted on with a cotton swab. Mother applied a dressing of egg white on the area of the sore several times a day until it healed. There was something about the protein-rich egg white that restored the damaged tissue, and I healed. I had a daily dressing of it for years afterwards whenever it began to get sore. By the time I had

103

completed 20 years of teaching, I had been absent only 27 days, and 11 of those were not for illness but for funerals, conferences, or workshops. My health was excellent.

In the Elgin school system salary raises were given for both experience and additional college credits earned. I watched for extension courses at local schools that would broaden my background as well as give me salary credits. In the summer of 1964 I took a course in supervising student teachers though I secretly wondered if I would ever be asked to take a student since my methods of classroom management were a bit unconventional.

In 1968 I was asked to take my first student teacher. In the next 10 years I was asked to take six in all, and I accepted five of them. I considered it a privilege to help build their confidence and perfect their skills, and it was payment of the debt I owed my own cooperating teacher. All were delightful, sincere young women unconcerned about the things I had worried about, like the fact that I taught sitting down or didn't use the blackboard. All five were offered positions in the Elgin system, and three took them. Years later I had the chance to visit the classroom of one. She taught that day almost exclusively sitting at her desk. She could have worked either way, and I certainly didn't feel she was less effective because she sat. I began to notice in my own building how often teachers sat, and I decided that secondary teaching especially could be adapted to a sitting position and still be of high quality. Many teachers proved this daily.

When I began teaching, I wanted desperately to succeed. I accepted another of Dr. Hook's obligations—to write professionally. Partly I did this because I wanted the recognition as if to prove my competency. Maybe this was a natural reaction to those people who felt I could never teach. I know a few parents expressed concern that their children would be shortchanged in my classes. I *had* to do a good job and be worthy of my chance. I was not really recognizing that it was God's strength being perfected in my weakness, and I was too caught up in what *I* was doing. Of course, I thanked God for giving me success, but I still concentrated on looking as good as I could.

During my career, a gradual evolution occurred. I became less interested in how I looked. Instead I wanted my students to look good and also our whole school staff as a group. Part of this development was prompted by a series of courses that stressed more humane approaches to teaching. Part was due to my growth as a Christian. While changing trends, shifting values in education, and declining interest in excellence invaded classrooms, I saw my teaching change from skill to art. I tried to become more conscious of everything I did and to justify my actions. Disciplining privately and avoiding sarcasm helped me build respect. Giving students chances to change and telling them they could be better helped me save a whole class I had grown to despise. Basically, just caring for each and every student and encouraging them all made me a better teacher. I adapted the prayer of St. Francis of Assisi to express my thoughts.

Lord, make me an instrument of learning.
Where there is hatred, let me foster understanding;
*   where there is self-doubt, confidence;*
*   where there is malice, concern for others;*
*   where there is apathy, involvement;*
*   where there is potential, responsibility;*
*   and where there is a lack of ability, self-acceptance*
*   and a sense of worth.*
Make me remember always that I teach young people first
*   and subject matter second.*
Make me remember always that each student is an individual
*   precious to You*
*   with individual contributions and individual needs.*
Help us grow in mutual respect and trust.
Give me the humility to recognize that in guiding others,
*   I truly teach,*
*   and in their learning, I am rewarded.*
Send me the courage to fight the good fight;
*   forgive me when I fail;*
*   and bless us every one. Amen.*

Teaching has been a wonderful career for me. At times it has been hard, demanding all my resources. There were years when the school was overcrowded until an additional junior high could be built. Some years I was responsible for more than 250 students a day in five classes, two study halls, and a homeroom. At least one year I taught four different subjects a day — two classes of ninth-grade English and classes of seventh-grade English, social studies, and reading. Yet I can't imagine any work that could have been more rewarding for me than working with young people. Whole families of brothers and sisters have been my students, and eventually I taught second generations as their children came through junior high school.

Over the years my teaching position enabled me to serve a variety of students and share their life experiences: two potential suicides, a class of problem ninth-grade boys, gifted children, student residents in the local mental hospital, and Indo-Chinese refugees.

I felt the students nearly always accepted me. Some, in fact, wanted to shower me with love and attention through their own natural generosity. They would ask when my birthday was, and I knew they wanted to do something special. I do not celebrate my birthday anymore. My state of dependence already makes me too indebted to too many people that I don't want my birthday to be another extra day for doing things for me. Nevertheless, two girls baked me a sheet cake in the shape of Snoopy and celebrated my unbirthday. Sometimes there are Christmas presents, a few cookies for my lunch, the first spring flowers, or dozens of thoughtful things to show their affection. One year a whole reading class planned a surprise party on our last day together. They lured me to the office and quickly decorated the classroom and set out refreshments in my brief absence. The all-boys class and I went to lunch together (Dutch treat) at a nearby restaurant. We have shared many good times.

One group of ninth graders in a first period class took to answering my "Good morning, people" greeting each day with "Good morning, Miss Bramer" in unison. It was only a few days before they began singing to me the whole little song each day, our private tradition. I was ill one late winter day, and I sent in lesson plans for a substitute. I didn't mention the singing because I didn't know what they would do. About 10 that morning Mother answered our doorbell at home and signed for a Western Union telegram. There it was:

> Good morning to you,
> Good morning to you,
> Good morning, Miss Bramer,
> Good morning to you!
> First Period Class

As miserable as I felt, that telegram picked me up. I went back the next day and thanked them. They were most disappointed to find out it hadn't been sung; they had collected money and ordered a singing telegram!

What good times they gave me. Quite often I think they forgot I was in a wheelchair. Often someone would say something like, "Why were you standing by the office after lunch today?" I never *stood* anywhere, but I had been sitting there. A few times as a battery became old, I'd find the wheelchair losing power during the day. I would send a student to bring the battery charger from my storage closet and connect my wheelchair to it and the charger to the wall outlet in the classroom. This restricted my mobility greatly, but I could still work from my teaching table. Students entering the class were quick to size up the situation and offer such chipper comments as, "Oh, I see your're getting a charge out of life," or, "Do you have that run-down feeling?"

As my original wheelchair wore out after 10 years, I bought myself a new electric one for $1,300. I was proud to pay for it myself with money earned teaching, just as I always paid for repairs, new motors and batteries, and all hand-splint repairs. Since it was a faster chair, I took the new one to school. The students noticed the different chair at once and were curious to know what was better about it. They wanted to see me do a "wheelie" with it. Of course, the novelty wore off the first day. Several weeks later, though, I got the idea that my feet would be more comfortable all day if the pedals had carpeting on them. Dad glued on pieces of indoor/outdoor carpeting, which prompted one of my favorite comments. One boy spotted the change instantly. "Aha," he said "wheel to wheel carpeting!"

Lest I give the wrong impression, I must admit teaching hasn't been constant joy. No job is. I have chafed under certain administrative decisions. I have suffered through some staff misunderstandings. I have had antagonistic students who resorted to vandalism. I have had disrespectful students. I have been threatened with physical violence. Several unhappy girls stated their intention of kicking me out of my wheelchair, pushing me downstairs, and breaking my legs. One of them left my study hall most days saying, "I hope you *die* tonight!" Because age and deeper faith have made me a much calmer person, these words didn't seriously bother me. I preferred having her anger directed toward me and not fellow students. Many students have had deep hurts.

After I had been teaching several years, Dad indulged himself in a fantastic luxury. He bought a used Corvette. The little car was his joy, although it soon become obvious he had bought a lot of problems with his used car. In 1965 he traded it in on a brand-new white Corvette Sting Ray. Only two could ride in it, and it had no trunk for a wheelchair, so it never replaced the family car. However, Dad loved it.

When Dad sold out his interest in the uneven partnership, he was not unemployed long. He went to work for a consulting engineer in a nearby town and drove back and forth each day in his Corvette. Later he took a job in town about a mile and a half from home. During this period my beloved taxi man John became ill and had to stop his taxi service. Since Dad worked in town, he began taking me to school at 7:45 on his way to work and picking me up at 5:15 on his way home. These were long days for me, but there were compensations.

Since I left a wheelchair at school and another at home, only I had to be transported each day to my job. This meant we could go in the Corvette. My status rose tremendously when I arrived and left school in such a neat car, even though there were few students around to notice.

In 1970 Dad retired. New possibilities opened. I could come and go at my convenience, attend meetings elsewhere in the district, and know I could get home easily if I became ill. Dad's car quickly became familiar to the students. It was not unusual to have a student pop into my room after school to announce, "Miss Bramer, your husband's here."

107

Some nights it would be announced my "brother" was there. Rarely did anyone guess him to be my father. Father seemed to look at least 10 years younger than his age. I always suspected, however, that the kids just assumed anyone as old as Miss Bramer couldn't have a father young enough to have a Corvette.

When I told Mother about it, I noted, "Either he looks awfully young, or I'm looking awfully old to have my father mistaken for my brother or husband."

"Does that bother you?" she asked.

"I guess not," I decided, "but when they announce my *son* is here to pick me up, I'll know it's time I quit."

Father took me everywhere. My height makes me awkward to handle, and I suspect some men fear they might hurt or drop me. In the early days one of my fellow teachers and Mr. Hulmes had transported me to some teachers' meetings, but that teacher had been promoted to a principalship elsewhere. It seemed Dad was always there and always willing. On the few occasions when he was unable to get me or take me to school, a cousin or a friend filled in.

When I graduated from college and began teaching, I didn't expect to continue college studies; I certainly never anticipated earning a master's degree. However, since salary raises were linked to earning additional hours of college credit, I began taking an occasional night class. These were courses I needed to fill gaps in my background. Often I was asked if I was working on my master's. I wasn't, but many colleagues began to advise me to get the degree — especially if I planned to be a career teacher. It seemed like too much effort unless I took off a year from teaching. I didn't want to do that.

After the triumph of Russia's Sputnik, much criticism was leveled at American education. In response the National Defense Education Act organized and offered workshops and institutes to improve the quality of education. Although the first grants were in the fields of science, in 1965 an NDEA Institute in English was offered at the University of Illinois during the summer. The credits earned could be applied toward a master's degree. Since I knew the campus would be convenient for me, I applied and was accepted. Once again Mother journeyed with me back to campus for the eight-week summer session. I began a program toward the advanced degree. The plan worked beautifully. In the summer of 1966 Mother and I returned to campus for the summer session. In 1967 I worked from home on an independent research project and completed the degree requirements. In August of that year, I was awarded a master of education degree.

My career-teacher status seemed obvious. Even so, during the next 10 years I continued to study, taking whatever courses offered new materials or new insights into education.

The discipline of studying was good for me, helping me remain mindful of what it takes to be a good student. By the time I had earned 32 hours beyond the master's degree, it became almost impossible to find courses I could still use that were offered in convenient places, but I felt I had strong, full majors.

Keeping up was important in order to be the best teacher I could be. Teaching has been an ideal career. There have been very few occasions when I have needed any help that students haven't been able and willing to provide. Junior high school students are very capable. They have given me a purpose for my life and richly satisfying work. How great is the God who made all of it possible! Truly, my soul sings.

How great Thou art; how great Thou art!

Something for Thee

Striving! I was always striving to accomplish something. My handsome, healthy, helpful brother had died, and I had lived. Somehow I had to justify my existence.

A well-meaning friend had once asked me about my illness and my brother's. When she heard how I was unconscious in an iron lung at the time of his death, she said sadly, "Too bad you couldn't have died, too." I knew what she meant. She felt so sorry for me in my dependent state that she felt the best solution would have been my death. I know many people felt sorry for my parents, weighed down with both the sorrow of having a crippled child and the burden of her care. More than one member of the family must have felt like the uncle who advised my parents against ever bringing me home from Warm Springs. I knew too that I had been the first to get polio — the disease that had taken my brother. Even if he didn't die from the same type of polio that I had, no one knew how the disease was spread or if one source could cause both kinds. I very well may have infected him with the disease that killed him. Knowing that, I felt an extra need to make some sort of positive contribution with my life.

At first, getting my high school education seemed to be enough of a goal. After all, I wasn't very strong, and studying was taxing for me. I did rejoin the church choir, and Dad took me faithfully to choir practice whenever he was in town. I was also asked to solo occasionally at local churches. Although I was always nervous and edgy about performing, I loved being part of other people's worship services. It seemed I was using the talent God gave me for His work. The few times when I was paid for this singing, I sent the money back to the churches at once.

When the national Easter Seal organization established a center in Elgin, Mrs. Jeffrey, the newly hired therapist, was given my name by someone. She was seeking local crippled children to offer them treatments and their families a mutual support group. Since Mother gave me whatever therapy I needed, Mrs. Jeffrey had no services to offer. What she did give me was far better. She gave me the chance to *serve*.

She asked me to write the appeal letter for the fund-raising campaign. I did, writing it as if one of the little patients was speaking. She also had me write some local press releases. It was then that Attorney Franklin Kramer, president of the local association, invited me to be a member of the advisory board. That began one of the most pleasant associations of my life. For 18 years I served the local chapter. I maintained their mailing list as a paid employee for $10 a month. I offered to do it for free, but Mr. Kramer insisted I be paid so that I might earn some social security credits. I was moved to the board of directors and served several terms as secretary and one as vice-president. No one on that early board ever seemed to consider whether I could do some task or not; they just gave me tasks to do.

I left the Easter Seal Association when the focus changed. The direction moved from local independence to united fund raising and government grants. Mrs. Jeffrey was gone, and the new director found fewer and fewer uses for me. I quietly resigned before my happy memories turned bitter.

I became active professionally. When the Illinois Association of Teachers of English held its annual conferences at the University of Illinois, attending was like going home for me. One year Beryl went with Dad, Mother, and me; one year I was a workshop speaker. This organization published my first writing—another obligation Dr. Hook taught his teachers. Later I wrote for the *English Journal, Learning* magazine, Bantam Books, Scholastic, Harper and Row, and Houghton Mifflin—some for money and some for free, some signed and some anonymously. I also wrote curriculum materials for my own district and gave workshops.

It was always important to me to feel that I had something to contribute in life. A handicapped person is by the nature of his infirmity sometimes forced to be a "taker." That was not a role I liked nor accepted well. Even as a very young child, Mother said I never liked being fussed over. I never wanted to be carried once I could walk. I would have chosen to live my life not being ministered unto but ministering, had I been given the choice. Unfortunately, my circumstances limited me dreadfully.

My love of history led us to join the local historical society as a family. Except for church, this was the only group to which we all belonged together, and we enjoyed the common interest. In a short time I became the secretary of the society, and the board meetings were held at our house. I served for two different presidents—both great historians who made every board meeting a lively event. As the

1971 anniversary of the Chicago fire approached, the president brought a book on the fire and suggested we each read it. I had it first, read it, and passed it on. By summer as we planned our September meeting, it became apparent that I was the only one who had completed the assignment and read the whole book. Reluctantly I let myself be persuaded to present the program and began doing serious research, sending for reprints of the old newspapers of the day. I made a series of overhead transparencies of a Chicago city map that would be projected on a screen, showing the progress of the fire in two hour intervals.

The Monday before I was to give my presentation, Dad took me to the public library for one final check on facts to corroborate my research. The new library was completely accessible for the handicapped, but the city parking lot next to it was not. Dad left me on the curb while he took my papers and went to unlock the car. I hadn't realized how close I was to the edge until the chair started to roll and tip off the edge. Dad saw the movement and spun around to catch me as I began to fall from the chair and the chair tipped over. Somehow Dad was able to catch me before I hit the ground and, holding me, was able to right the chair, which had fallen sideways. He set me in it, and I complimented him on his fine catch. "You can play on my team any day," I told him, grateful that nothing worse had happened. I thought I was unhurt although my left leg had doubled under me in my semifall. Later at home as Dad lifted me from the car to my power wheelchair, there were twinges of pain, but nothing seemed wrong. By the time I was ready to go to bed, the whole knee cap area was swollen, and moving the leg the tiniest fraction made me cry out in pain. I had torn the ligaments in the knee.

Years earlier I had suffered a similar, though milder, injury. Dad had been taking me to night class when the car ahead of us came to an abrupt stop in traffic. We were not going fast, and Dad hit the brakes, stopping before he hit the car ahead. However, this was before we owned a car with seatbelts, and I was catapulted like a rag doll from the front seat, crumpling under the dashboard where I was wedged in. Dad pulled the car to the side of the street, got out to come to my side, and tried to lift me back onto the seat. I was in such a position that he could not move me without hurting me. Before he could decide what to do, the door on the driver's side opened, and a long-haired young man in a black leather jacket reached in strong arms to help lift. He had been lounging against a building and had seen the whole incident, and when Dad explained that I was crippled, the young man became angry. He wanted Dad to chase the thoughtless woman who had stopped and could still be seen proceeding on through town. Dad was more interested in giving the young man some money for his help, but he refused and just walked away. By appearance, much of the world would have judged him a hoodlum, but he was like an angel to us in our time of need. I went on to my night school class, but when Dad came back later to pick me up, both knees hurt and were mildly swollen. Ten days with hot compresses and aspirin took care of the problem.

Although only one leg was involved, this time was much worse. I must not have much tolerance for pain because this injury hurt intensely. Since I have no control of the leg, it fell by gravity whenever Dad picked me up, sending tearing pains across the knee. Mild pain pills did not blur the pain enough, so the doctor prescribed stronger medication. By carefully timing when I took the pills, I could get up and get to school through all the movements those operations entailed while the drug masked the pain. Once seated at school, I could remain still enough to get through the day. Midafternoon I took medication again in time for it to take effect by the time I had to return home and have the leg handled for the second compress of the day. Getting to bed required the same careful timing, and I tried to sleep with my leg immobilized on pillows. By Sunday, the day of my Chicago fire presentation, I was getting along fairly well. An audience of history buffs must be one of the best in the world to address, and I was glad I saw it through. By the time I gave my talk for a neighboring historical society, my leg was well.

The need to eliminate architectural barriers (like the parking lot curb where my wheel chair tipped) led me to accept a place on a committee sponsored by the YWCA. We knew at the end of the year that we had really only made a beginning, but we had fostered greater awareness of the needs of others. A similar goal led me to work with a group seeking better minority housing, and briefly I was an active member of the American Association of University Women.

These activities added a dimension to my life. It was good to mix and work with people outside of my teaching staff and to feel that what I was doing was worthwhile. I had often joked that my favorite Bible verses were Luke 14:13 and 14. In them people having a dinner are advised to invite the cripples, for these cannot make recompense. Certainly such acts would highlight the generosity of the hosts, but the inability of cripples to make an equal contribution was clearly emphasized. The knowledge that I could no longer carry my share of responsibilities has been one of the hardest aspects of being handicapped.

Before I became crippled, I liked being helpful. I loved it if my piano teacher would let me stay after my lesson to straighten up her apartment. I probably never helped at home anywhere near as much as I should have, but anywhere else I was the first volunteer. I remember helping my teachers at school and wishing I could do even more. I used to wish for something extra to do when I babysat.

After polio I still wanted to help, but it became much harder to find things I could do. I wanted so much to be of service. Until I began teaching, I was a faithful choir member, but as a teacher I could not commit myself to a night a week for rehearsals plus Sunday mornings. I had thrown myself into teaching and all its satellite activities. Often I came home from school just short of exhaustion, occasionally going right to bed and not getting up until the next morning. I missed the interaction at choir though.

In junior college I belonged to the young adult group at church. When the pastor wanted a project for them, I suggested a late Christmas Eve service. I planned the service, using young people almost exclusively — a ministerial student from our congregation, ushers, musicians, and an art student for the bulletin cover. From the choir loft, I faced the congregation, their faces lit with candle glow as they sang "Silent Night." How breathtaking it was to hear the voices proclaim "Christ, the Savior is born" as the organ chimed midnight.

Years later I felt the church should do something special for the Bicentennial. Thanksgiving, the only national holiday based on a religious *and* historical tradition, seemed appropriate. I wrote a family service for Thanksgiving Eve. The parish parochial school children spoke, relating what Americans had to be thankful for. The whole congregation sang "America, the Beautiful" with an added verse:

> We thank Thee, God, For this good land,
> Our land of liberty,
> For all the blessings Thou has sent
> To build democracy.
> Now bless all those who labor here
> To keep this nation free,
> And bless the cause of all who work
> For peace and unity.

Both of these services have become regular parts of the church's calendar although I have not written any more of them. For the congregation's 40th anniversary I planned a Heritage Sunday, wrote the church's history, and sang in the reunion choir. It was a joyous event, a day to remember.

Even in less spectacular projects I am convinced that great satisfaction comes from serving the Lord. The years I was on the church's long-range planning committee doing quiet, background service were so rewarding. To be able to help someone in need financially or send a small gift to a widow for her first Christmas alone lessens my sense of being crippled. So many kind things have been done for me that I feel deeply in debt to others, in some cases to people now dead whom I felt I never repaid properly. Thus, doing for someone else is like keeping an unbroken chain of kindness going — a service of love for the Lord.

114

Give me a faithful heart, Likeness to Thee,
That each departing day Henceforth may see
Some work of love begun,
Some deed of kindness done,
Some wand'rer sought and won,
Something for Thee.

"Some wand'rer sought and won" is the thought that makes every area of my service in life questionable. I know that my highest service of love is to bring others to the knowledge of God's love and the Good News of salvation through Jesus Christ. Here I know I fail. I fail to speak so often. I become cowardly and mute. I, like Peter in the last chapter of John, declare my love for Jesus, yet I hesitate to follow the commission so clearly given as the response of love—to feed His sheep and lambs.

In my maturing years, especially in my Bible study groups, I grew keenly aware that being a Christian was not a passive state. Living a "good" life and attending church are piously shallow. A Christian must be actively working for God. Pastor Ross told one Sunday of the Scandinavian church that had a fishing net hung on its wall. When asked about the reason for the net, the members always explained it was to symbolzie their purpose to be fishers of men. But Pastor Ross told his congregation that it was time the members took their net off the wall and put it out where the fish are. He challenged us to accept our commission and go out in our own worlds to work for the salvation of others. If that is the purpose for which my life was spared, then I still have work to do.

Just As I Am

For many years after I began teaching, I remained active on the local Easter Seal board. I knew in 1963 at the annual campaign kickoff dinner that I was going to receive some kind of recognition, but I wasn't sure exactly what. Unknown to me, Mrs. Jeffrey had applied for a national Gallantry Award for me, and the board had instituted a local award for a handicapped person. Mrs. Jeffrey knew us personally and had no trouble making a guest list of relatives, friends, and school associates to invite. Mother knew some of the details, but not all, and she was pledged to keep everything a surprise for me. I knew I would be expected to make some sort of acceptance speech, and public speaking was always nerve-racking for me. The dinner was to be on a Thursday night after a full day at school for me.

To complicate matters, I was suffering that week with very painful feet. I had been to a podiatrist for routine care. He had painted the cuticle with a medication to which I was allergic. Long, pencil-like blisters appeared next to the nails on both feet. When my toes were compressed in shoes, these swollen, blistered areas caused excruciating pain. It was almost impossible to force shoes on my feet, and I cried with pain until the toes went numb and I could bear the discomfort. Coming home from school with John that evening, I confessed my misery and anxiety and told him I didn't think I would go to the dinner. In his easy way he encouraged me, "You might as well go. You got through school all day. It wouldn't be any worse." Little did I suspect that he and his wife Beryl were on the guest list and would be there.

When I entered the house, I knew there was no turning back. Mother was quite excited, though she was also concerned about my suffering feet. A box containing a beautiful orchid corsage had been

116

delivered—a gift from Mr. Thompson, the superintendent of schools. How had he known? Later at the restaurant, I found I was to sit next to Mr. Hulmes, my school principal, and his wife. I hadn't known they were coming either, and there were several others from school. Guests also included several relatives and even Mrs. Stewart, my former voice teacher. I was overwhelmed.

Mr. Hulmes was master of ceremonies for my portion of the evening. He spoke of his reservations at having me on his staff, and I learned for the first time that Attorney Kramer had not been my only advocate in getting my job. John Van Arsdale, my faithful taxi man, had stopped by Mr. Hulmes' office early that summer of 1960 to speak on my behalf. According to Mr. Hulmes, John had argued that I had worked so hard to get my education that I deserved a chance. Since John's wife was already on the staff, he had a pretty good idea what teaching English involved, and he thought I could do it. That may well have been the persuasion that tipped the balance in my favor and convinced Mr. Hulmes to accept me. I had never known of John's efforts before.

Then Mr. Hulmes introduced Mrs. Thompson who was representing her husband, the superintendent, who had obligations elsewhere. She apologized for his absence and asked Mr. Hulmes to read publicly a letter from him. It began with congratulations on overcoming a handicap and went on:

In addition to a physical problem, she [I] had the handicap of encountering people who underestimated her abilities—who didn't think she could make it

Somewhat shamefully, I recall the many times I tried to discourage Mary from teaching. Along with others, I tried to persuade her that she couldn't possibly assume the responsibilities of a classroom teacher. At one time, and I hope Mary will someday forgive me, we sat in her living room and were almost cruel in telling her we had to employ teachers on their merits, and merits alone, and that teaching of children was too important to be considered just a job that one could get if enough pressure was applied.

He remembered as vividly as I, but he was wrong in suspecting I held any malice. Once he had given me the chance to teach, I only wanted to justify his action and be a good teacher. His public apology reduced me to tears as Mr. Hulmes continued reading. I was given a beautiful plaque, mumbled some words of thanks, and once more dissolved in tears as the guests gave me a standing ovation. Somehow I said thanks to all those who congratulated me, posed for a newspaper photo, and survived the evening.

My feet were still in agony when we got home, and when I removed my shoes, the first of the shiny blisters broke. I soaked my feet in a medicated solution, and more blisters broke at the slightest touch, bringing the first relief to my painful feet. I collapsed into bed emotionally drained.

About a year later I received a message at school to call home on my lunch hour. When I did, Mother said I had received a letter from the Warm Springs Foundation announcing I had been named Alumnus of the Year and would be honored at a ceremony on the afternoon before Thanksgiving. I was to be the foundation's guest and would be met at the airport in Atlanta. Mother and I had gone back for checkups twice before at Thanksgiving, which was always a special time at the foundation. She was already planning to go. I was pleased at the honor, but the bell ending lunch had already rung. I had to get to class. I told no one in the office, but I was bursting to tell someone. I looked at my dear seventh graders and decided they should know. I told them that I had just had a call from my mother and that I was invited to Georgia to receive an award. They listened closely, and when I finished, Greg raised his hand.

"Does your mother open your mail?" he asked.

I laughed. "I guess she does if it looks interesting."

"That's just what my grandmother does," he said. I could see we shared a common link in our domestic lives.

At first, taking time off from school seemed out of the question, but it had been 12 years since I'd been back. It would be good to have a checkup. I wrote for an appointment as an outpatient. As it would be Thanksgiving week, there would be only three school days to miss. My request for absence was granted. Those dear seventh graders gave me a silver charm with the award date engraved on it and a homemade card with individual messages from each of them.

Dad took us to O'Hare on Monday, and Mother and I made the flight back to Georgia. We loved the peace of that place but were amazed at how much the pace had slackened. When the vaccine conquered polio, the flurry and hustle ebbed at the foundation with fewer and fewer cases each year. We enjoyed the good food, the gentle weather of a southern November, and seeing those old friends who were still on the staff. On the day of the award, my school secretaries sent me a corsage, and the faculty sent a bouquet of red roses. Basil O'Connor, who had been Franklin Roosevelt's law partner, presented the award. I was the first woman to receive it, yet the joy of that day was far overshadowed by the medical benefits of the trip.

I had seen the doctors on Tuesday morning. They noted the increase in the curvature of my spine but were satisfied with the range of motion in my arms and legs. There had been some stiffening, for example, but my fingers could still be laid out flat. Then Dr. Bennett announced that he was going to prescribe a different handsplint.

"Why?" I questioned. I was always one to resist change.

"Because we have a far better one now for someone with your limitations," he explained.

"But I'm getting along fine," I countered. "I'm earning my living with this one. There's nothing wrong with it."

Fortunately, he wouldn't take *no* for an answer. He insisted I have one made while I was there. If I honestly didn't prefer it, I wouldn't have to pay for it. It was an offer I couldn't refuse. He explained that when the vaccines lowered their case load, the bracemakers had time to develop much better devices. This new handsplint was one of them. My old handsplint had a bar under the fingers in a rigid position. Each pen or pencil I used had to be fastened in a clip that then slid onto the bar. Thus in order to write I always had to have one of my own specially sheathed pens or pencils and be wearing the handsplint, which was otherwise useless to me.

The new splint was a marvel. It still fastened to my hand and wrist, but this time with Velcro pressure strips instead of small buckles. The new splint was not rigid and allowed movement of the wrist; in fact, it capitalized on it. The remaining muscle strands that allowed me to raise my right hand at the wrist were converted to an artificial pinch at my fingertips. Thus, I could pick up any pencil or pen (using the wrist muscle), hold it, and write.

After Billy finished making my splint, he gave me several tests to try its usefulness. Of course, I could not then and still cannot lift anything of any substantial weight, but I could lift a styrofoam cup of coffee, papers, small books, a purse, and various objects. When Billy dropped a dime on the floor and I could slide my fingernails under it, pinch it, and pick it up, I knew I had a very special handsplint. It opened up a whole new range of activities to me, including writing on the blackboard — or at least the lower portion that I can reach from a sitting position. It and the electric wheelchair have become the most valuable aids in my life, giving me some degree of independence.

These first awards made me feel good and rather proud. I had succeeded where I had been expected to fail. The awards proved it. However, as other awards came, I began to realize that I myself was doing nothing. Of course, I freely acknowledged the support of both parents in all my endeavors. God had given me dedicated parents. But I knew whose strength it was that prevailed in my weakness. God had blessed my efforts; I had been merely His instrument. I alone achieved nothing.

It had been a slow evolution from my early, competitive self, trying to win awards and scholastic honors, to my quieter, supportive self with my preference for background roles. I know that the only credential I have of any real, lasting value is that my eternal salvation was earned long ago by Jesus Christ. The labors of my hands and the awards of men have earned me nothing. Christ died for me just as I am.

> *Just as I am, without one plea*
> *But that Thy blood was shed for me*
> *And that Thou bidd'st me come to Thee,*
> *O Lamb of God, I come, I come.*

We Give Thee but Thine Own

The old familiar hymn said it so well:

> We give Thee but Thine own,
> Whate'r the gift may be;
> All that we have is Thine alone,
> A trust, O Lord, from Thee.

Oh, how I could have worked in this world if I hadn't been crippled! I could have sewed, played the piano, painted, designed, cleaned, visited, cooked, gardened, etc., etc., etc., helping everybody with whom my life came in contact—if only I hadn't been made so useless by such a crippling disease.

For a time I half believed that. Or maybe I just tried to convince myself because it was such a wonderful excuse. I looked at people with normal, healthy bodies, living somewhat selfish lives, and I thought to myself how differently I would live if I had a healthy body as they all did.

But that was all hypothetical. I did not have a healthy body, but I did have a body. I didn't have all the skills and talents I imagined I would have had, but I had some gifts. I might never be any better physically than I was at that moment, but I was alive. Then, quite obviously, the question became, What was I doing with whatever talents I had?

At first after I returned home from Warm Springs, I was jealous of everyone who had had polio and recovered. It seemed so unfair that some victims should get well while others did not. After all, everyone recovered from chicken pox, didn't they? And measles? Then logically everyone should recover from polio, too, but that was obviously not the case. I could cite an even greater example of unfairness. Why did just some people get polio in the first place? That gave me an even larger group of people of whom to be jealous. Fortunately, I never shared my pitiful jealousies, and it was not hard for me to see what an unproductive waste jealousy could become in my life. I was what I was; I would be only what God would have me be.

I knew too that the Scripture said quite plainly that to whom much was given, much would be required. Since I was not given much, or more correctly, since I was not left with much after the polio attack, not much would be required of me. But there was also the reference to being a faithful steward over just a little. I began to see that I had to live so well with whatever talents and gifts I had — no matter how little they seemed — that I could give a good accounting of myself. After all, if God had wanted me to paint or cook or play the piano or do something physical for Him, He would not have let me be crippled. Just the way I was, with exactly what He had given me, He expected me to be a faithful servant.

God had given me an ability to teach. Could I claim to be the best example of a Christian teacher that I could be? Of course not! After I went through a professional metamorphosis, I learned to emphasize the positive aspects of my teaching. I became aware that my attitude definitely influenced my classroom. I learned more positive ways to respond to students' needs. I practiced techniques for building students' self-confidence. I tried to show my concern for my students and their problems. They couldn't be on top of the world each day any more than I could, and many lived daily with problems almost beyond my comprehension.

As I changed, my students changed. The more love I gave them, the more they returned. It was a beautiful principle — almost like a scientific formula or a Biblical ratio — with blessings multiplying among us. The more I prayed over my teaching and the more I used classroom Christianity, the better the job became. Once again I felt as much joy in teaching as at the beginning.

My teaching job gave me a good salary, far better than I could have ever earned selling magazine subscriptions from my home. Was I using enough of it in God's service? During my school years I had faithfully tithed my earnings, but they had been so pitifully small. When I began receiving a decent salary as a teacher, I increased my giving greatly, but not up to a full tenth. The only money I truly tithed was what I earned from writing, the bonus beyond my regular salary. I supported my church with regular contributions. In addition, I selected a few charities and special Christian projects to receive my extra donations. Occasionally, I filled special needs at church, school, or the Easter Seal Center with some extra purchase. When a friend decided I needed a tape recorder and gave me one as a gift, I in turn bought one like it for our church school.

Since I didn't keep house or raise children I seemed to have a certain amount of time, although not always matched with strength. Did I use that time wisely? Did I always find time to listen to the problems of others? Can anyone answer such a question affirmatively? I know I did not always stop for visits from former students at school because I felt the obligation to my employer to be getting my work done. School offered a unique situation where former "patrons" came back to visit during "business hours." I know I failed to keep in touch by telephone and letter as well as I should. I didn't always get all the things read I wanted to or all the things done. Use of time was as hard to judge as to spend money wisely.

God gave me a quick mind. Had I used it to learn more of Him? Unfortunately, I did little more than attend church during much of my adult life. When my mother's afternoon Bible class moved to evening hours, I was invited to join. After a while, when weather problems sometimes kept me away, it seemed easier to move it to our house permanently. For over five years a group of ladies met every Wednesday to study the Bible with our patient teacher, so appropriately named Jewell. We studied individual books of the Bible, topical studies like witnessing and spiritual gifts, and various people of the Bible. We met regularly year round except for two years when we gave up Bible study during Lent. Too many members had services at their own churches and were concerned with falling too far behind the class, so we disbanded temporarily. Through that study, I finally began to see some Christian growth in myself. I know that the refinements in my attitudes and my growth in trusting God's future for me are results of that class. Bible study — especially in a group — was so much more instructive than reading alone. Over the years I have been in several other studies as well — each contributing to my understanding in its own way.

God gave me a love of words and of writing. He gave me a gift of song and a sense of humor. I should enumerate every trait and talent God gave me and then question my use of each for Him. Every examination would help me evaluate my use of God's trust. Rather than dwell on what I could do *if* I had certain talents, I had to acknowledge that I was as God wanted me to be. Therefore, I would be expected to serve Him with what I had. What a strange concept — no excuses to hide behind, no reasons for not serving. It was a new perspective to living.

Quite by accident one Sunday evening as Dad switched television channels, he tuned to a religious program broadcasting from Orchestra Hall in Chicago. We had discoverd the Chicago Sunday Evening Club. Each week guest speakers offered gospel messages complemented by beautiful music — soloists, a chorale, and guest

123

choirs—and testimonies of Christian living. I owe that program much.

Once John Haggai spoke on David's battle against the Amalekites to capture the families and possessions that had been carried off in his absence. Some of his men were so weary they could not pursue the Amalekites and stayed behind to guard the baggage. When David returned triumphant and began to divide the spoils equally among those who had battled beside him and those who had stayed behind, the warriors objected, feeling they alone had the right to the spoils. David insisted each deserved an equal share—those that went to the battle and those who stayed behind. John Haggai applied the story to show that everyone has a part, but the rewards are equal for doing each particular part well regardless of the part itself. I could see that my part was according to my strength and abilities and my reward according to the way I did that particular part to be the best of my ability. How simple! We couldn't all be front line warriors; some of us were too weak for such strenuous roles. Yet each of us had a part to do well. That, after all, was the secret of every good operation—each person doing well in each separate aspect of the whole. I needed to realize that.

Another message gave me another insight. Bruce Thielemann related how he had planned to drop out of the ministry just three months short of graduation. However, the professor he most admired visited his college room with this simple concept, "You think God called you to be successful. God didn't call you to be successful. God called you to be faithful." Those words kept Bruce Thielemann in the ministry. They also made me reexamine my purposes in life. My search for fame, for recognition, for some justification for my survival was not what God wanted of me either. What God wanted was my faithful performance of whatever He gave me to do, my faithful stewardship of His gifts.

Cardinal John Henry Newman had expressed similar feelings in the nineteenth century when he wrote, "God has created me to do Him some definite service. He has committed some work to me which He has not committed to another. I have my mission. I may never know it in this life, but I shall be told it in the next. He has not created me for naught. If I am in sickness, my sickness may serve Him . . . ." I felt a kinship with Cardinal Newman in his simple articulation of individual purpose chosen by God. God had His own plans for me; He did not need my direction. I never needed to ask for what I thought would be best for me; God already knew. I was already part of His plan.

Several years into my teaching career, a student shared a thought with me that touched me and has remained one of my favorites. She understood it to have been written by an anonymous Confederate soldier during the Civil War. I was told it was the creed of the Institute of Physical Medicine and Rehabilitation in New York City.

A Creed for Those Who Have Suffered

I asked God for strength that I might achieve;
I was made weak that I might learn humbly to obey.
I asked for health that I might do greater things;
I was given infirmity that I might do better things.
I asked for riches that I might be happy;
I was given poverty that I might be wise.
I asked for power that I might have praise of men;
I was given weakness that I might feel the need of God.
I asked for all things that I might enjoy life;
I was given life that I might enjoy all things.
I got nothing that I asked for, but everything
      I had hoped for.
Almost despite myself, my unspoken prayers were answered.
I am, among all men, most richly blessed.

God truly had given me everything I needed. I was what I was by the grace of God. The gifts I had to return to Him were the ones He had entrusted to my stewardship. I never needed to ask for miracles before I could serve Him, for I was only expected to serve with what I had, to perform the tasks He had planned for me.

What a Friend
We Have in Jesus

The steward stopped at each pair of seats along the narrow aisle of the small plane. "Now what?" I wondered out loud.

Mother leaned across me to look at the steward's face as he spoke with the passengers in the front seats. "Something's wrong," she said.

Something *else*, she should have said. The trip had been plagued with hardship since our arrival at the Atlanta airport early that morning. The confusion was more than the usual Thanksgiving holiday crush. Posted on the departure board was the notice our flight had been canceled.

Mother had gone instantly to the harried clerk, our tickets in her hand. "What's happening?"

"I'm sorry, ma'am, our flight engineers went out on strike this morning. We have had to cancel your flight."

"But what can I do?" Mother pressed. "I'm traveling with my crippled daughter."

The clerk's eyes flicked beyond Mother momentarily to where I sat in a wheelchair with a white-uniformed attendant beside me. "I am sorry, ma'am. We will get you on a later flight just as soon as possible. All of our smaller planes are flying. We will try to get you on an afternoon flight to Chicago. Please be patient; we will page you just as soon as we have seats available."

Mother relayed the grim news to me. I had ridden to Atlanta by car instead of by ambulance as on the previous checkup visit. My precious sitting-up time would be eroded by any delay. I looked at the attendant who had driven me from the polio foundation at Warm Springs. "Do you have to go back now?" I asked.

"Oh no," he said, "I won't leave you 'til I've got y'all on board that plane—if it takes all day!"

That was bleak comfort. If it took all day, my weak back would give out, and the tissue-thin skin covering my sharp bones would be worn raw and painful. An all-day wait was beyond my endurance. We sought a place to lie down in the crowded airport, but the lounges were all divided by chrome arm rests between the individual seats, even in the washrooms. Had I come by ambulance, I would have had the ambulance cot.

"I'll call your father," Mother said, "so he won't be leaving for the airport before we're off the ground here." She waited in one of the long lines at the phone booths and returned to us with more bad news. "It's snowing in Chicago. He said there's not much accumulation yet, but several inches are predicted."

We joined one of the long lunch lines to get something to eat. I ate a part of a sandwich but risked nothing to drink. The wait took most of the day. In the late afternoon I was carried aboard the small plane and set in the last aisle seat. Changing my seat brought momentary relief, but I was already miserable and hurting. Mother had called Dad to give him our new arrival time. It was still snowing, but he promised to be at the airport to meet us.

The flight was not the nonstop trip of the original, bigger plane. Instead we would make stops in Birmingham, Nashville, Louisville, and Indianapolis before Chicago. We would be arriving at eight o'clock in the evening instead of one in the afternoon. The first stop was uneventful, and we took off into a sunset sky that blazed in coral and orange above us. In Nashville slivers of ice pelted the plane's windows and glazed the runway beneath us. As we sat in the cold cabin, a voice announced over the speaker, "The Louisville stop has been canceled. The Louisville airport is closed due to ice on the runways. Passengers with a Louisville destination are advised to debark and seek ground transportation."

Mother looked at me. "Do you want to get off?"

My reply was instant. "No! What would we do here?" What was she thinking of? Who would carry me off the plane? Where could we go?

"Are you afraid?" she asked.

"No." Was she? Flying was not common in the early 1950s. It was her fourth flight, my fifth. "Mother, they won't even take this plane up if they aren't confident they can make Indianapolis. They won't risk this plane and passengers."

Later I wasn't so sure. The Indianpolis stop had been a lengthy one as ground crews scraped ice off the wings. Sometime after 10 we took off for Chicago. The "Fasten Seat Belts" and "No Smoking" signs had been on for what seemed like hours, but had probably been only 20 minutes. I peered steadily through the plane's window on Mother's left, searching for the lights of Midway Airport. All was blackness and swirling snow just beyond the glass.

Now it looked like more bad news as the steward approached. He stopped by our seats with his terse message, perfected by repitition. "We are turning back. We don't have enough fuel to continue circling the airport until it's our turn to land. There are too many planes stacked up, and we can't wait. We bucked a terrific headwind all the way up, and now we're going to try to take advantage of it as a tail wind. We're going to try to make Indianapolis."

I was in tears before he finished speaking. I had been unable to go to the bathroom, straighten my legs, or get the pressure off my thin skin since early morning. It was close to midnight. Frustration and discomfort overwhelmed me. I couldn't endure any more. Irrationally, I wanted someone to open the cabin door and throw me out. Dad was down there somewhere beneath me; he would catch me. I only wanted to be safe in my father's arms.

Safe in my father's arms—literally and figuratively! While I longed to be reunited with my earthly father knowing he would take care of everything, it was impossible for me to do one thing about it. When I became crippled, I was placed in a totally dependent state. This condition was bearable because of the devotion and care of my parents. But I was in anguish, nearly frantic with discomfort. Dad was beyond reach, and Mother could not honestly offer me any help. Even if we made it to Indianapolis, we knew no one there to help us. We would be strangers in a strange city. I had to relinquish my fate to God.

All day I had prayed. My early morning prayers had been for a safe, routine flight. As the troubles of the day shaped our actions, I prayed for an early flight, for the snow to stop in Chicago, for the strength to endure. As my strength ebbed, I prayed for help with the pain. As the weather worsened, I prayed increasingly for the pilot and crews, for all those who worked on such a night, and for Mother and me. At last I gave up directing God, telling Him what I wanted and needed. If He had spared me in all my illnesses and had me survive polio only to die in a plane crash in a raging blizzard, so be it. I had to admit there was not one force around me that I could control. My tears continued, but they were tears of physical agony. Inwardly, I was calm and totally unafraid. I was safe in my Father's arms.

Meanwhile in the passenger terminal at Midway, Dad had been spending a frustrating evening watching the arrival board as the times posted next to our flight number were changed again and again. When the midnight arrival time was erased and no new time posted, Dad took action. The airline employees could not, or would not, tell him anything. He quickly went behind the counter and through some authorized-personnel-only doors and demanded to know where our flight was. He was just being told to get out when someone with more authority listened to Dad's reason for asking — his wife and crippled daughter were on board.

"Tell him," the authority said. "He has a right to know."

Dad was told the truth. The plane would not be landing in Chicago. Low on fuel, the pilot was trying to make it back to Indianapolis instead. There was nothing Dad could do and no reason to wait. He also had to relinquish the whole situation to God — that and fight the continuing blizzard and deepening snow as he drove home alone to Elgin.

The threat of common disaster united that cabin of 30 strangers in a common goal — to get to Indianapolis. A few passengers knelt in the aisle and prayed. The Jewish couple in front of us turned around and introduced themselves. They were returning with the couple ahead of them from a Florida vacation. Seeing my tears, they asked how they could help Mother and me. Mother quickly explained that I was crippled and suffering considerable anxiety at the moment. Thinking I might be worried about money to spend the night in a hotel, they offered financial help. Mother assured them we had enough money. Then for her sake they offered to make arrangements as soon as we landed to get me into a hospital for the night. In fact, they offered anything we might need — contact with the Travelers' Aid, help getting train accommodations to Chicago, a hotel room, whatever. They promised not to leave us stranded at the airport. Suddenly, arriving at a strange city in the middle of the night in the midst of a storm didn't seem so threatening.

In fact, others were ready to help, too — the airline staff. When we touched down safely, the crew swung into action helping everyone. A young man in a yellow slicker beaded with ice came on board, carried me down the steps to my wheelchair, and hustled me into the nearly deserted terminal. We were told the airline would put us up at the Indianapolis Athletic Club. We rode into town in the limousine with the pilots. At the Athletic Club the only open entrances had revolving doors. No one was available to open them flat, but someone suggested the loading door at the service entrance in back. At last we arrived upstairs in a room with a beautiful bed and bathroom.

Mother's strength became superhuman as she struggled to get me through the narrow bathroom door and finally into the bed. It was well after 1:00 A.M., but we were down, safe, dry, and warm. Mother tried to call Dad, but there was no answer. Could he still be waiting at the airport? She called Aunt Rose and woke her. She couldn't believe we were in Indianapolis, as she and Uncle Bill had been past our house earlier in the evening. They thought we were home and in bed since there was no light, but our driveway was shoveled—a courtesy of the Smiths who realized we were overdue getting home and had wanted to welcome us. Aunt Rose promised to have Dad paged at the airport and get back to us.

There was nothing to do but wait. Within a half hour the phone rang. It was Dad. Aunt Rose had missed him at the airport but was calling at home as he came in the door. He wanted to get right back in the car and drive to Indianapolis to get us. He was sure the main roads would be open. After the exhausting day he had put in, he was ready to push himself to get to us—night driving in a snow storm! Mother insisted he go to bed. We had been promised seats on the first flight for Chicago in the morning. She said we couldn't sleep if we knew he was on the road. That persuaded him; we all needed some rest.

We awoke to a cloudy morning, but the snow had stopped. Mother went down to breakfast and met our friends of the night before. They had made train connections and offered to do the same for us. Mother declined but thanked them for their help and support. We were told to be at the airport by 10. Bright sunshine broke through on the fresh snow, but inside the terminal there was still much confusion. The strike continued with the added burden of storm rerouted passengers waiting to complete flights.

I was pushed out on the runway to be carried on board first, but no one came. Airline personnel began boarding other passengers. My despair must have shown on my face, for a young soldier stopped to inquire into our distress. He told me not to worry; he would get me aboard. He bounded up the steps into the cabin, but the last aisle seat was aleady occupied by a woman who refused to give it up. Boarding through the tail made this a choice seat—the first to exit. When the soldier explained his need, the person one seat ahead willingly gave up his aisle seat. The soldier picked me up as if I weighed nothing and dashed up the steps with me in his arms. Mother wanted to pay him, but he refused. When we arrived in Chicago, Dad was there to carry me off.

The trip had been an ordeal, but also an exercise in trust. We had come through safely. When we felt most powerless and alone, God had sent perfect strangers to meet our needs. To my knowledge I have never seen any of these people again, yet each was there to provide what we needed before we asked it. Yet that early example of a loving, caring God came to a slow maturity in me. I was so slow to let God help me.

My life has always been blessed with good people, far outweighing the mean and petty ones. We have had good neighbors, good associates at work, good fellow Christians at church —all sharing their friendship. However, it was in establishing friendships that I found one of my hardest adjustments.

One of the greatest shocks in my altered lifestyle after polio was

130

the loss of friends. Those young people with whom I had played, attended school, worked, and shared the ragged years of childhood disappeared from my life almost completely. Nearly all of them came for at least one token visit for old time's sake, but the enormity of my disability became an unbreachable gap between us. Their lives and mine no longer touched on common ground.

I began to realize how different my life had become, a fact I had really known since returning from Warm Springs. I learned that the best-intentioned people — even my parents — could not guess my true feelings. I think I also began to realize that my personality was different from that of many other crippled people. For example, I always liked back-row seats at performances, feeling that the wheelchair was too conspicuous and I too tall. Others would love the front row. I was developing my own sense of belonging in situations where I felt comfortable.

Mrs. Stewart sensed my need for friends my own age when she asked Sue to accompany me at voice recitals. Sue was a marvel. She used to round up friends to come to the house to play bridge with me. These were nonthreatening social encounters in my own home. I enjoyed hearing Sue and her friends talk of their lives and eventually their loves. These bridge games continued through college years during breaks and until Sue married and moved a half a continent away.

Moving to our new house was traumatic. We were positive no neighbors could replace the Nelsons, and no one ever really did. Yet we had good new neighbors, too. Phyllis, Al, and Becky became close when they bought the new home across the street. Becky was with us often, especially if no one was at her house after school. Phyllis, like Aunt Rose or my cousin Lois, sometimes stayed with me a few hours when Mother had to go downtown on errands. During those early days before I had an electric wheelchair, Mother hated to leave me home alone since I could not push my own wheelchair. I was willing, but Mother worried that I might need something. When Mother returned, Phyllis always stayed on until well into the dinner hour. She joked about her culinary skills and would leave only minutes before Al was due home. "Just time to make creamed eggs again," she would say. Creamed eggs became our idea of a meal of last resort.

One night when Al was to be away, Phyllis invited me for dinner so I could try creamed eggs. Eating away from my parents made me nervous, as I could not cut meat nor handle a beverage glass. But these were understanding friends, so I accepted. Mother pushed me across the street and up the step into their house and left. When dinner was ready, Phyllis alerted Becky (about a second grader at the time) to freshen up my hands. Becky came with a damp washcloth and towel as if she'd done it every meal for years. Creamed eggs proved very easy to eat—no cutting at all, and Becky put a straw in my glass without my asking. I had a delightful evening out—one of very few away from my parents.

I felt guilty about being so tied to my parents. I had become their sole responsibility. Their social life usually included me, as their friends planned events I could enjoy, too. We seemed to do everything as a family. Mother's desire for a long train ride prompted her only vacation away from me. Before good rail service to Denver was discontinued, Mother and Dad accepted an invitation from Dad's former boss to visit Denver. Our good friend Mrs. Lunn came to stay with me and care for me. Although only a few days in length, the trip was a wonderful change for Mother, her one vacation in 30 years.

Since Mother even went with me to college, her only other break from me was when she was hospitalized for a few days. I went to stay with Aunt Vange. Because her husband was an undertaker working from a chapel downstairs at their home, he was always around to lift me. Aunt Vange took care of my personal needs. I had always loved going to their house. One day each summer I visited them. My three younger cousins (all boys) and I played games together. Aunt Vange often played the organ so I could sing, but the highlight of the day was shopping. She lived only two blocks from downtown, and she and one or two of the boys pushed me through the stores. We browsed the dime store, the hardware or dry goods store, and always the wonderful bakery. After supper I returned home—Mother's one day off a year.

I don't know when I first knew that the best way to have a friend is to be one. I suppose as soon as I understood it, I accepted it, but until it became difficult for me to be a friend, I never thought too much about it. When it became evident in my late teen years that my peers and I were in different worlds, there was a definite void. The fact that my parents' friends often included me did not totally fill the need in my life. Friends should do things together, go places together, share problems and secrets, be active forces in each other's lives. Like so many aspects of my normal, healthy life, I had taken friendships for granted, too. As a young adult, I missed friendships in my life although I never expressed the emptiness.

My former school friends were dating and eventually marrying and starting families. They had mainly dropped out of my life earlier, but the gulf between us widened even more. I recognized that marriage should not be part of my future. I told myself never to fall in love, just as I told myself not to complain about my handicap. I thought I could have a disciplined heart, one I could control and order not to respond.

Suddenly, quite unexpectedly, into my life came Doug. I met him at Warm Springs where he was a patient when I returned for my

132

first checkup. He was kind, intelligent, sensitive, perceptive, and charming. As an absolute bonus, he was also handsome and — wonder of wonders — interested in me. I thought he was unique to be such a serious, knowledgeable young man.

As I think of it now, Doug's lifestyle and mine were almost polar opposites. He went at life full tilt, while I held back. If someone invited Doug on an adventure, he went. The same offer to me would have me searching for plausible excuses to decline. Doug took risks; I cherished security.

Yet we shared so much — our spiritual base first, a common polio experience, high ethics, music, humor, a certain scholarship, ambition, and a desire to serve. Doug's plan was to earn a law degree, mine was to teach. In our few days together we each sensed a responsive quality in the other. We promised to write and did — often.

His letters were so well written, eventually hinting at more than the actual words said. Was he obliquely asking if we might have a future together? I was afraid to risk being wrong and answer in kind. What if I was presuming too much? I would appear an aggressive female, coming on too strong. I might scare him away, and I wanted him as a friend. I don't think I ever wrote except to reply to him. It would have been too forward of me. My letters were shallow things, surface accounts of my nothing activities.

I thought of him often, and he gave my days a rich warmth, a texture of being cared about by someone who did not have to choose me for a friend. Because I was young and foolish, or because I was human, I thought about being in love with Doug. It would be so easy. Yet nagging always at the back of my mind was the certain know-ledge that I was not good enough for him. He was much less crippled than I, had much more to offer, and was far more mature. I banished the foolish dreams of love and marriage and just treasured his friendship.

At the thought of his first visit, I was torn. I wanted to see him, yet I feared he'd changed. I hoped he was still interested in me, yet I wondered what I'd do if he became serious. I wanted him to be in our home, yet I wished we still had a dining room in which to entertain. I worried about what to wear, what to eat, what to say — worry, worry, worry! He would be coming with a friend. What if the friend wouldn't like me? Doug had never met Dad, since only Mother had been with me on the checkup. What if they didn't like each other?

The fellows arrived — Doug and his friend Dana. Doug was just the same, or maybe even better. We had a joyous visit. Dana had as keen a sense of humor as Doug. They brought me a present — an invisible dog, Freddie. Freddie was the kind of pet even Mother would allow me to keep.

Quickly the time fled, and Dad came home from work. Mother

had prepared one of her generous meals and had improvised a dining table with two card tables set together in the living room. Dana practiced his Emily Post and carefully turned the dinner conversation to Dad. "What do you do for a living, Mr. Bramer?"

For some impish reason my father said, "Oh, I can't tell you at the table."

"Really?" Dana mused. "What can it possibly be?"

Dad allowed himself to be teased into revealing his mystery occupation. Finally he said, "I'm a sanitary engineer, Dana."

I always think people aren't sure what kind of engineer that is. Lest they think that meant one who washed his hands a lot, I interjected, "He designs sewage treatment equipment."

Since Dana seemed to be thinking it over, Mother felt compelled to help the explanation along, too. "It may not sound like much," she said, "but it's been our bread and butter."

What an unfortunate choice of idioms! Dana, who was eating a piece of dark rye at the time, dropped his bread automatically. I wondered if we had just committed the faux pas of the day, but of course we hadn't. However, there were a few references to kinds of bread in Doug's subsequent letters.

Despite the rollicking verse Doug wrote lamenting the state of his garden, he had the soul of a poet. When moon exploration was first openly suggested, he offered to reserve a trip for me (but not one of the first, which were most likely to fail). He would suggest sharing the anniversary of our meeting or a New Year's Eve by us both doing the same thing at the same time though miles apart. An evening at home alone for him might prompt his Bach recordings and a letter to me. Valentine's Day was never forgotten, but never conventional either. In fact, one year he sent a Valentine's Night greeting as the day had kept him too busy.

We didn't call long distance. We were both too practical, realizing someone else was paying our phone bills. Money was always an underlying concern. Doug's geologist father seemed to change his work often, and there were three other children in the family. Doug was always trying to earn the money necessary to support himself in school. Once he worked as a radio dispatcher. He learned bookkeeping and kept several private accounts. He had consulted the Division of Vocational Rehabilitation in various states where the family had lived, but nothing dependable ever worked out. We had an understanding that gifts between us would be unnecesary. I could never afford to give him what he deserved anyway. Also, I didn't want him to feel obligated to remember holidays or fear I might judge him by the value of his gift. Instead, his economies were inventive and humorous, making a package from him a delightful surprise.

Doug's college work never went smoothly. He had the academic ability to do well, but he took an overload every semester hoping to finish early to cut expenses. Sometimes he lost a semester due to a family move or a period of hospitalization. Because I had pledged to myself not to lay my burden on anyone else, I rarely wrote about any disappointments. I did write once that I was discouraged because I was not allowed to take a full load of college work. He replied that he was not as far along as he thought he should be either. He suggested we both live a couple of extra years to make up for it.

As I wished and yet feared, Doug was serious about me. In fact, he wanted to marry me. He was willing to wait until we both finished college, but he wanted to establish a home. He would be a wonderful husband and father, but I knew I would be a poor wife. I felt marriage was difficult enough between two "normal" people without complicating it with handicaps from the start. Maybe I was too timid, but I knew what my answer had to be for both our sakes. When Doug proposed, I declined, gently, I hope, because I was conscious of what an honor it was to have a good man want me for his life partner. Our friendship continued for seven years in all. Ultimately, I kept my disciplined heart; Doug gave his to someone else. I hope he was blessed as he deserved.

Almost 10 years later when I was working on my master's at the University of Illinois, I met an interesting fellow teacher. He too was in a wheelchair, but again far less handicapped than I. Our relationship deepened from being casual fellow students into strong friendship. Once again I set very careful, obvious limits to keep it at friendship only. Time has not made me regret my decisions.

As I grew into the "old maid school teacher" category, I began to pretend that I was on a desperate search for a husband—if only I could find one rich enough and old enough or ill enough. Whenever the newspaper reported the death of any elderly tycoon, I always lamented that I hadn't met him in time. That attitude seemed to put most people at their ease. My jokes about finding a rich husband became family jokes as well.

I don't think I missed romance in my life, but I did miss the companionship of a steady friend. The loneliest were the high school years when I was tutored at home alone. Without brothers and sisters, with no close cousins, and without even a pet to fill my time, I devoted myself to school work. In night school college classes I met many fine people but made few lasting friendships. No friends came from correspondence courses, obviously, and my time on campus at the University of Illinois was very brief.

To be fair, I must admit I probably made it hard for people to be friends. From childhood on I had been rather independent and never needed to be with people. I had always loved reading—a marvelous solo occupation. After my polio restrictions, I could still fill my time by myself, especially since I was slow at things. I hated to talk about my personal limitations, so it may have been difficult to judge what I

135

could or could not do. Rather than get me involved in an uncomfortable situation, it was easier for people to exclude me from the start. I never admitted what I longed for because I never wanted people to do things for me out of pity.

When I began teaching, I intended to be nice to all my associates, but I didn't expect to mix socially. For one thing, I had little stamina left over. However, there were 14 new teachers the year I began, a natural nucleus for social gatherings. We joined a staff that had already begun its own convivial traditions. Parties, picnics, and potlucks were planned. Dad took me when I went, although sometimes another teacher or teacher's husband would bring me home. Since I could not transfer from my wheelchair to a car by myself, I tried not to ask people if the purpose was only social. For almost 30 years I held to that policy, preferring to stay home rather than put someone else out. I never wanted any party idea scrapped just because the restaurant or person's home was inaccessible to me or the activity was impossible for me. I was not anxious to be a social albatross.

Mother went out of her way to entertain on my behalf. The faculty women came for summer luncheons and evening bridge games, and the single teachers held potluck suppers on our porch. One of the nicest aspects of socializing with my school staff was the number of times my parents were included. An evening of travel slides at a teacher's home included my folks, too. Sometimes one or two teachers and their spouses would dine out together with my parents and me. In fact, one dear mathematics teacher and her husband became close friends of my parents — especially after she retired. This was a bonus in teaching I never expected to find. Just as my parents' friends had welcomed me years earlier, my friends welcomed my parents as well.

Entertaining at home always required hours of preparation for Mother. As she became older, I felt guilty about letting her entertain for me. Once or twice I had parties catered at home, and many times we entertained at home with prepared foods. Eventually, I applied for a social membership in the local country club so that I could plan my own entertaining and repay my social obligations without burdening Mother.

Donna, a fellow teacher, sensed another desire I had. I could not go shopping alone. After I no longer spent a day with Aunt Vange, only my parents took me shopping. Dad was never a shopper and operated on the take-the-first-thing-you-see-and-get-it-over-with theory. Mother was more patient, but she met so many people she knew that we spent more time talking than shopping. Donna changed all that. She loved to shop and suggested the idea. What's more, she was my size and could try on clothes for me. I usually had to take things home to try them and frequently had to return them.

Donna's way was better. It was a great day when Dad dropped us off at Spiess Store and I did my first Christmas shopping for my parents without either one along.

After some painful attempts at friendship as an adult, I adopted a facade of independence. I felt I had many associates and acquaintances, but few (if any) real friends my age. During the period before my spiritual reawakening, I was often cynical about life in general and my own life in particular. I reasoned that nobody needed a crippled friend. Cripples were a drag on the friendship market. A friendship with a cripple would be too one-sided—the cripple always receiving with little or nothing to give in return. Thus, I told myself, if nobody needs a crippled friend, I would never force my friendship on anyone.

Donna entered my life. I knew that friendship was fragile and rare. I tried not to rush it. I waited for her. When she dropped in one Sunday afternoon, Mother invited her to stay for supper. From then on she often joined us, rounding out our party when we went out to dinner, plays, exhibits, and flea markets. We had many common interests. We were both well into middle age, both unmarried, and both in agreement on so many philosophies. I felt truly blessed. For the first time since polio struck, I felt comfortable referring to someone as "my good friend." God must have sent her into my life.

Then Donna began dating a man and devoting all her free time to him. At first I pretended nothing had changed, but I was puzzled and hurt that she no longer had time for me. I prayed that our friendship would endure, but I awoke many nights from troubled sleep with tears streaming down my face. Like the psalmist David, I literally cried to God in the night watches. I saw Donna slipping from my life, and knew the situation was beyond my control. Years earlier in an airplane cabin I had to consciously yield the situation to God and trust Him. I prayed, "God, You know I miss her, but I will accept whatever is best for Donna."

Giving my loneliness to the Lord and trusting Him for both my future and Donna's, I began to find peace. By the time she became engaged, I had accepted my loss completely although I still missed her. She had become like the sister I never had, but I lost her as surely as I had lost my brother. But Donna left me by choice. I began to appreciate even more the words of the familiar hymn:

> What a Friend we have in Jesus,
> All our sins and griefs to bear!
> What a privilege to carry
> Ev'rything to God in prayer!
>
> . . . .
> Can we find a Friend so faithful
> Who will all our sorrows share?

Jesus knows our ev'ry weakness —
Take it to the Lord in prayer.

. . . .

Do thy friends despise, forsake thee?
Take it to the Lord in prayer;
In His arms He'll take and shield thee,
Thou wilt find a solace there.

What I found was better than solace. How could I have doubted? I had often heard that the Lord never takes away without giving something and that God's gifts are better than an earthly father's. After losing my mobility, I sometimes questioned that reassurance, yet He had given me my wonderful parents. This time He gave me two friends to replace Donna.

Doris and Bill were great to be with. Dad enjoyed Bill's masculine interests without conversations dominated by the women's viewpoint. Doris did so many helpful things for Mother. Their only son was grown and away from home, and they took time to do so many nice things for me. For the first time I began going places without Dad always taking me. Bill was not afraid to lift me in and out of a car and collapse the portable wheelchair to take along. Both of them enjoyed shopping, and Doris was also my size. Our most restful vacation days were spent visiting at their cottage in Wisconsin. What joys their lives have added to ours. The Lord richly blessed us all.

Through the years I have enjoyed some very special friendships. Mrs. Lunn, my cousin's mother-in-law, was a precious friend until her death. No one ever spelled Mother and gave her a vacation until Mrs. Lunn stayed when my parents went to Denver. She lavished care on me those few days. She had been a widow many years and had supported herself and raised her daughter with her skills as a seamstress. Since getting clothes to fit my irregular size and special needs was always a problem, Mrs. Lunn came to my rescue again and again. She could take a pattern from a garment that fit me well and copy the style to make me a new outfit. She adapted patterns for me. She and her daughter Fran surprised me with gifts of clothing, since they nearly always had my measurements at hand. During the early days after polio when I often sang at weddings, I searched for a suitable dress. Mrs. Lunn asked me to pick fabric, and she set to work. I chose pale yellow with a white floral pattern that she worked into an attractive dress with a little bolero jacket. It was my summer "best" dress for years until I gained enough weight to outgrow it. How often my appearance was better because of these two.

When I grew to accept myself as a person, I learned to accept friendships in whatever degrees they were given. I tried to be a supportive, sharing, forgiving, and helpful friend. One of the most understanding collections of friends was the core of the Bible class to which Mother and I both belonged. Our gentle, loving teacher knit us into a cohesive group that truly shared. We prayed together through personal joys, tragedies, and crises. Yet even these special Christian friendships are transient — ebbing, changing, realigning.

In retrospect, I can see it was never easy to be my friend. I hated my dependent state. My early decisions not to complain about my physical condition and to mask my inner feelings may have cost me. It would have been more honest to indicate my wants, but I never wanted to elicit pity. My independent spirit came from both parents. My mother took care of me and her household so well that no one thought to help her. Dad so willingly transported me everywhere that no one offered to relieve him. We became a tight family unit blessed with counterbalanced strengths, and we survived.

One noon hour a young substitute joined our teachers at lunch. He told how his father had made the army his career and his family had moved often. He went to say, "I attended nine different schools before high school."

Someone asked the obvious. "Didn't you have a hard time making friends?"

"Not really," he said. "My best friends were always my family." He went on to explain. "We met nice people wherever we lived. We always joined a church, but the happiest times were always family times."

I understood exactly, as my life had taught me much the same. He had voiced what I had long felt. I often thought how I would have enjoyed doing things with my parents had we been contemporaries. We had no generation gap between us. My greatest earthly blessings were my Christian parents who were also my best friends. If I ever needed an example of faithful friends sharing trials and temptations, my parents have been it. Through it all, supporting us all, has been the love of Jesus — the best example of a caring, sharing, burden-bearing Friend.

Have Thine
Own Way, Lord

I had the premonition that I was going to get polio, but I never suspected that I wasn't going to recover from it. I had often been sick, but had always gotten well again. From the start, though, polio was different. First, my brother died from it. Always before I had had my illnesses alone, or if someone else had a touch of what I had, it was always a lighter case than mine. Second, the aftereffects of polio were so obvious and so devastating. Clothes had hidden my inch-and-a-half-wide hernia scar. Glasses did not necessarily indicate my years of eye problems and surgery. In fact, I always looked pretty normal—even when I'd been very sick. But polio was definitely different.

The early months dragged on with little or no improvement. My therapist at Warm Springs had told me I would never be better, but I had thought she was wrong. Yet the months dragged into years and the years into decades. With the passage of time, my once-straight body deepened into a most obvious spinal curvature. The eye that I mentally ignored in order to live with my double vision began to stray further and further upward in its socket. My always uncertain breathing grew more raspy and ragged with less and less provocation. Stiffening and tightening set into my limbs, and my range of motion narrowed. No miracle occurred; no medical breakthrough resued me. It appeared that I would be confined to a wheelchair for a lifetime sentence.

I didn't ask why about my life, because I was as capable as anyone I knew to provide the earthly answers. I accepted it at first because I believed it would be temporary—a few years at most. In high school I wrote a little verse that mirrored my feelings:

> *Unable to hear great music, oh, God, that is too much;*
> *Unable to see the flowers, to only smell and touch,*
> *Unable to sing Thy praises, to me that seems unfair.*
> *My cross is that I cannot walk, but my cross I can bear.*

I knew that most people had some cross to bear, and I honestly believed mine was tailored to fit me. I also trusted that even my severe crippling would serve some purpose and ultimately would work for good, as St. Paul assures those who love God. The challenge was to live with my handicap with as good grace as possible. The little serenity prayer spoke to me.

> *God, grant me the serenity to accept the things*
> *   I cannot change,*
> *the courage to change the things I can,*
> *and the wisdom to know the difference. Amen.*

The things I could change were my personality and my relationships with others. I could maintain a positive attitude of optimism. I could look for the good in others and minimize the faults. I could become more tolerant, loving, and forgiving. I could not change the degree of my paralysis one bit. I would have to be crippled and dependent as long as God permitted it.

Another sermon by Bruce Thielemann telecast by the Chicago Sunday Evening Club helped me shape my philosophy more fully. He preached on the text, "Bear ye one another's burdens" (Gal. 6:2). This was not a suggestion, he said, but a command. In order to bear we must first share. This was another revelation to me. Instead of hiding or minimizing my limitations, I could acknowledge them freely and accept help. Just as I was given a crippling handicap, others had been given the responsibility to help me. Just as I shared my burden, I should try to pick up the load of someone else — perhaps just by being a listening ear or an encouraging friend. There was a marvelous interweaving implied between those with needs and those to share them. It had never been easy for me to be my parents' "burden," as many thought of me. Being a burden erodes self-respect. Yet being a burden to someone and a burden-bearer for someone else hinted at a fine balance.

Recognizing that God intended the lives of His children to be complementary made it easier to accept my dependence and my limitations. I knew that God's strength "is made perfect in weakness" (2 Cor. 12:9). I also knew that I had to submit myself to Him. A simple hymn expressed the relationship so well.

> *Have Thine own way, Lord, have Thine own way.*
> *Thou art the Potter, I am the clay.*

Mould me and make me After Thy will,
While I am waiting, Yielded and still.

As far as I know, Clarence Darrow, the famous trial lawyer, was not a Christian. However, he propounded a metaphor for life that has had much impact on me. He compared life to a game of cards played uncomplainingly. He stated that the game may not be worth the while nor the stakes worth the winning, but the game should be played bravely to the end. I disagree that the stakes aren't worth winning, for the Christian knows the prize at the end. I do accept the rest of the metaphor. Life can be compared to a game of cards. The cards dealt are not the result of random chance, but rather the result of God's plan. Each player must play the best game he can with whatever cards he's been dealt. Every hand cannot be a winner or one for the record books, but every hand merits being played well. Each player has the obligation to play the best game he can in the best way possible.

This has not been the life I would have chosen for myself, but I have accepted it. It has not been a cruel, spartan existence, but a life rich in blessings. It has not been a lonely life because I have shared it with my precious parents and many fine people whose paths have crossed mine. It has not been a useless life because teaching has been such a satisfying career. It has not been an empty life because God was and is always there.

Learning to Lean

Writing an autobiography obligated me to review the events and circumstances that shaped my life. Since the purpose of this writing was to make a Christian witness, I had to put my spiritual life in order, too. I can't remember not being a Christian. Going to Sunday school and church were always in my family's schedule. At my confirmation I consciously renewed the vow made on my behalf at my baptism: to be faithful unto death. I think perhaps my main idea of God at that time was that He was a watchman and knew everything I did. At times this probably saved me from committing some sins, but it was not a concept guaranteed to insure my good conduct.

After I contracted polio, I was told that my illness was a sign of God's love. Such a sign brought little comfort. I struggled with secret guilt because I had become ill first with the disease that killed my brother. Had he caught it from me? Was his death my fault? I prayed often—thousands of petitions to get well—yet I didn't get better. I asked, but it wasn't given unto me. My understanding was limited and confused.

As I began to mature, I recognized that my relationship with God was very shallow. At one time I read the entire Bible through, but I felt no wiser for having done so. Until I began to study the Bible I found very little growth in myself. I began to find consistency in the Scriptures. Each Bible class built on the knowledge gained from the previous one. Sermons became more meaningful. There was a sure basis for everything in life, and I began to apply what I learned to my own life.

My family seemed to have made all the major decisions before I was an adult. However, I had decisions to make in my classroom—many that gave me anguish before I learned to give them first to the Lord in prayer. I had to put into practice exactly what the song said:

Learning to lean, learning to lean,
I'm learning to lean on Jesus.

This meant casting every concern on Him from the smallest to the largest. Finding a good winter coat has always been a problem for me as I could not use a long coat, yet I wanted something dressier than a jacket. When I began teaching, I found that a fur jacket was the best solution, and I bought myself a squirrel jacket the first year I taught. When the squirrel became so badly worn that it could no longer be repaired, I began looking for a new fur. I didn't want a heavy, bulky fur, and my choice was almost limited to rabbit, which would wear out quickly, or mink which was too fancy and expensive. I couldn't justify $2,000 for a coat, but the furrier said squirrel jackets just weren't available. For over a year I looked whenever I was in a store. Was finding a coat too unimportant to pray about? Lord, you know my needs; help me.

One day in late summer I received a phone call from a friend. Her husband and I had taught together for several years, but they were moving to Florida. She wanted to know if I could use her fur coat. "It's just a fun fur," she said, "very light weight, but very warm. I'm taking my mink, but I won't need two fur coats."

Could I use it? She was a tiny person, and the coat had to be restyled slightly to fit me. Everything else was perfect. She refused to let me pay her anything for it, although it was almost brand new. It was, of course, an answer to prayer.

Living closer with God has changed me gradually. I search for the good in people and situations, even when I'm being critical. I care more about people, and I feel a reciprocal response. I see changes in the people around me because I myself am somewhat changed. Although I backslide, I can always start again, and I do. I have come a long way on my spiritual journey. The greatest evidence is my growing trust. My future is especially uncertain as my parents grow older and increasing health problems plague me. However, there is great consolation in the knowledge that I am not making this journey alone.

One night on the Chicago Sunday Evening Club Martha Hoke told of the crisis in her family when her oldest son lay unconscious in a hospital room following a traffic accident. The doctor had told her and her husband that their son had suffered back injuries that might leave him unable to walk again. The Hokes prayed that night a complete prayer of trust, "God, we'd rather have a crippled son who walks with you than a physically well son who doesn't." Her words made me think about another alternative to being crippled—being well and godless. With that alternative I too would pray Martha Hoke's prayer. To walk with God is more important.

Micah (6:8) summed up concisely what God expects of us—"to do justly, and to love mercy, and to walk humbly with thy God." I cannot even remember how to walk anymore. Sometimes when I'm on hall duty at school, I watch the students passing by. I try to see just what position the left foot is in when the right foot is raised from the floor to swing forward. I try to see just when the weight shifts from the heel of the foot forward to the ball of the foot, but it is too complicated. I cannot follow the intricate timing visually. Literally, I cannot walk, but figuratively I walk each day with my Lord. In the last few years I have shared a closer walk, learning to lean on Him, knowing He will carry me completely when I need Him most.

One night some time after this story had been started, I was facing a desk full of papers to grade, but I couldn't keep my mind on my task. A verse of Scripture raced in and out of my mind, linking with other ideas and multiplying them. Suddenly the words began to form in short, rhyming patterns. I took pen and paper and hastily scrawled them down. As I wrote, notes of melody sounded in my mind, and I could hear a whole song. When I was through, I had a gospel song and a statement of my faith. I sang it into a tape recorder so I wouldn't forget it. Only then was I able to attack that stack of papers and get on with my school work. This is that song.

My child, I am with you;
there's no need to fear.
Through all of your lifetime
you know I'll be near.
I'll share ev'ry sorrow;
I'll wipe ev'ry tear.
My word is your comfort
when trials appear.
Remember, My child,
whatever you do,
My grace is sufficient for you;
My grace is sufficient for you.

Remember I loved you
and made you My own,
Prepared you a place
in My heavenly home.
I earned your salvation;
My love I've made known.
Now I walk beside you;
you're never alone.
Remember, My child,
whatever you do,
My grace is sufficient for you;
My grace is sufficient for you.

Through valleys of shadow
you know I'll be there
To lighten your darkness,
your burden to share.
I'll never send more than
I know you can bear;
I'll listen whenever
you call Me in prayer.
Remember, my child,
whatever you do,
My grace is sufficient for you;
My grace is sufficient for you.

This is my story; this is my song.

I Can
Face Tomorrow

When I began writing this autobiography in the summer of 1980, I had just completed 20 years of classroom teaching. It seemed an appropriate time to examine my life, to sort through the debris of my memory, and to inventory my years of living. I expected the experience would be sometimes traumatic, often tedious, and alternately sad and joyful. It was all of these and much more.

In the beginning I dreaded most reopening the thinly healed wound of my brother's death. Each August it is difficult to get through the days when Mother announces the anniversaries of his death and then of his funeral. Generally, we do not talk about this, as we have said everything there is to say; going over everything again serves no purpose. Yet I had to face that time in my life in order to write honestly and completely.

At the time of his death, I was in an iron lung not expected to live. In fact my own death had been erroneously reported in the local newspaper. I did not know this until after I was home from Warm Springs. One summer day Mother showed me a newspaper clipping with the shocking headline: MARY BRAMER DIES OF POLIO. At first a quirky thought shot through my mind—I was dead already! But obviously the crippled state I was in was neither good enough to be heaven nor bad enough to be hell. The newspaper headline had been a mistake.

Mother explained what had probably happened. In those days the paper had a one o'clock deadline for the afternoon edition. There was no local radio station. My brother had only been admitted to the hospital that morning and had died by noon, so his illness was virtually unknown outside of the immediate family. Apparently the newspaper called both hospitals each day just before press time to get the current facts on the polio epidemic. In that dreadful plague week there had been almost a death a day and several new cases to report in each issue. The hospital had probably reported a Bramer death and may even have correctly given my brother's name. It is also possible that my name had been given in error, or that the newspaper had no record of any Bramer hospitalized with polio except Mary and had jumped to the wrong conclusion. Of course, the error was corrected the next night, but by then the dreadful truth had spread widely on the grapevine circuit.

Then Mother told me that Pastor Schuth had made a copy of Sonny's funeral sermon since I had not been present at the service. He had given it to Mother for me to read later when I was stronger. Mother offered me the message to read that day, but I declined. In fact, I declined steadily over the years whenever she mentioned it again. Thirty years had passed when I began this book, but I had not yet read the sermon. I knew it would reduce me to tears, and the terrible, aching loss would just be brought to the surface again. I decided just to begin typing my feelings.

I knew that I wanted the hymn "Be Still, My Soul" as the chapter title. I began by recalling vividly the details of the doctor's visit that I had never shared with another soul. As I typed, the tears streamed down my face, and the possibilities of what might have been had he lived overwhelmed me. He had not had the paralytic type of polio, and those whom we knew who had survived with tracheotomies had eventually gotten rid of their breathing tubes and returned to normal living. How much different my parents' lives would have been had I died and he survived! We had to accept his death, but I knew that as long as any of us lived, we would miss him.

When I finished my chapter, I felt an obligation after all these years to read that sermon. I was already emotionally drained. Mother gave me the typed, yellow sheets just as Pastor Schuth had given them to her years before. The text was "Be still and know that I am God." One portion of that sermon follows, a section that seemed to speak to my thoughts:

"Be still and know that I am God. I kill and I make alive; I wound and I heal." The Savior adds, "Are not two sparrows sold for a farthing and not one of them shall fall to the ground without your heavenly Father, are not ye much better than they? But the very hairs of your head are all numbered." If not even a sparrow falls to the ground without His will, did your child, purchased by the precious blood of His Son, fall at this time without His divine permission? You did everything possible for him, and yet you say, "Could we have done more to keep them from this contagion?" "Be still," He says, "and know that I am God, I kill and I make alive, I wound and I heal."

Don't you see it in this case? He says. Mary appeared to be the weaker, and you thought she, if any, would be the one to go; Alvin was the stronger, and yet he is the one who has been taken. See, He says, it is all up to Me. Your times are in My hands. Whom I wish to let live, no plague or disease can destroy; whom I would take to myself, no human effort can prevent or delay.

There it was — a strong reassurance that even though I had polio first, I had not caused Sonny's death. It was God who decided he would die and I live.

The same envelope held folded tablet sheets in Mother's hand-writing. It was the speech she had given at the Palmer House in Chicago. I had never heard or read it. When I told her what I'd found, she was unaware that she had saved it. It was her personal account of those first dreadful days when polio had decimated her family. Her account of my brother's death was much as I had been told, but her perspective on having her only two children stricken with such a frightening illness was different from mine. She had given this speech at the same meeting where she had heard State School Superintendent Vernon Nickell speak, saying that no child should be denied an education because of a handicap. Years later it was the memory of his speech that drove us to seek his help in gaining entrance to the University of Illinois. When he was approached by our friend L.D. to intercede on my behalf, it is just possible that he too remembered the speech of the mother who told her personal story that day. Her words were compelling.

I sincerely hope that polio will never touch your family or your loved ones, but should it ever come close to you, what you learn this afternoon may enable you to help others and to understand what they are going through. Please consider my true story as coming from the heart rather than the head.

Polio struck our family in August of '49. It had been a terribly hot summer, but life was going on as usual for the Bramers. We were exceptionally busy— painting our home, doing a lot of canning, etc. Sonny, our only son, was working for one of our local florists. Mary, our only daughter, was working as a page at the library and baby-sitting at night. All of us were taking an active part in our church's anniversary, looking forward to so many happy, full days. Our son had graduated from high school with honors and was leaving in September for the University of Illinois hoping to become a structural engineer. Our daughter was looking forward to her first year of high school, dates, dances, etc.

Then polio struck! Mary's symptoms were a severe headache and fever. She was taken to the hospital by ambulance and placed in the isolation ward. Our family physician was positive it was encephalitis (sleeping sickness) plus spinal meningitis, but hated to admit the possibility of polio. His suspicions were confirmed by Dr. Tornabene, our county's polio doctor, when he finally got to check Mary. He was so terribly busy during that epidemic, working many hours without the benefit of sleep. Needless to say, the props were knocked right out from under us when the doctor came to the house to inform us. You always think it can never hit you, but it did! How helpless you feel when you can't even go to visit your child. There was no miracle drug waiting for polio victims. There was nothing they could give Mary that would check the extreme fever or halt the advance of the disease. There was as yet no preventive and no cure, but we could pray, and pray we did. There had been no known contact with any known cases. We could only conclude that she had lowered her resistance by overwork and too many activities.

Two days after Mary's illness was diagnosed as polio, we received a letter from Mr. Schnell, our county chairman, offering assistance in any way possible and telling us an iron lung was standing by should Mary need it. The manner in which the assistance was given was wonderful. It didn't in any way make us feel as if we were a charity case. It certainly restored our faith in the goodness of people. We had known before polio struck how expensive illness could be. We had experienced sickness many times in our family.

Our doctor kept us well-informed on Mary's case, but things moved too fast! On Monday morning I was summoned to the hospital because Mary had become completely paralyzed during the night and was not expected to live through the morning. I called my husband home from work in Chicago. My pastor came to the hospital, too. Mary was indeed gravely ill. She didn't speak to us or open her eyes, but she lived through the day and night. Before we could get to the hospital on Tuesday morning, we were again summoned as Mary had been placed in an oxygen tent with no hopes for survival. The hospital was overcrowded with polio victims and short of nurses, so we stayed on with Mary wearing gowns and masks and sterilizing our hands, etc. At noon Mary was placed in a respirator, and believe me, friends, it is not a pleasant sight. On the other hand, you are thankful because it is helping your child to breathe. Where there's a spark of life, there's hope. You also feel everything possible is being done, yet you yourself feel so helpless. We were heartbroken, needless to say.

Wednesday morning our son complained about not feeling well and being so tired. We thought, no, he couldn't possibly be getting polio. Why he is six feet two and weighs 195 pounds and has never been sick. Surely, his stomach is emotionally upset because of Mary. In spite of their brother-and-sister tiffs, they thought the world of each other. Just to be safe, we called the doctor. He was very concerned and said he would watch him closely. He was out three times, gave medication, and prescribed rest in bed. Sonny put in a very bad night. We were up all night so the doctor came early in the morning. He was taken to the hospital with a throat paralysis setting in — bulbar polio. In less than two hours we were summoned again to the hospital. We knew it must be that Mary had passed away, but it was our son. The doctor said he had done everything he could for him, but he had filled up so fast there wasn't time for a tracheotomy. As the hopes of our lives came crashing down, my husband and I were almost crushed. We decided that day with the help of God not to become bitter if we could help it. When your children have twined

150

themselves around your heart and become part of you, you find it very hard to come home to an empty house. It is harder still to find their belongings where they left them and to realize your son will never return and your daughter's completely paralyzed, fighting for every breath in an iron lung, perhaps never to sing again or take an active part in life. You feel you have lost everything you hold dear. We wondered which was harder — to see our son in a glass sealed casket or our daughter in a respirator.

Mary was not informed of her brother's death for six weeks as the doctors thought that if she should become panicky, it would be fatal. It was very hard to go to the hospital every day and evade such questions as: Why doesn't Sonny come to see me? Is he at college now? Why doesn't he send me a postcard at least? It was at times like those that our faith sustained us.

About this time she was becoming stronger and opening her eyes. She had suffered a facial paralysis also, and her left eye wouldn't stay open. She couldn't receive hot pack treatments as she was too weak. One day she said to me, "Mother, I learned about polio in school and how much it costs to be in an iron lung. How is Daddy going to pay for all this?" I assured her all our bills would be paid. She smiled for the first time since her illness, and I will always maintain that the worry of money off her mind helped her tremendously in her fight to get out of the lung. Also, when Mr. Bramer and I were relieved of financial worries, we could help greatly in Mary's readjustment to her complete helplessness. Heaven knows, we had a heavy burden to bear, and if it would have been necessary to mortgage our home or lose it completely. . . well, all I can say is the NFIP is wonderful!

When the time came (of necessity for fear the news would be broken to her bluntly by some nurse or aide), Mary was informed of her brother's death by the doctor and our pastor. She took the news like a good soldier. When I arrived in the afternoon for my daily visit, she said, "I know about Sonny. We love him, but God loved him more." What a load off my mind! Such beautiful acceptance I had not expected.

Mother's speech continued with her account of my initial rejection at Warm Springs where it was felt the severity of my handicap would defeat the purposes of the foundation. However, caring friends interceded for me, and I was finally accepted. The diagnostic muscle test given on my entrance there confirmed that I didn't have one normal muscle left. Mother said that having lived with polio for six months, she and my father were prepared for the verdict. She praised my care there and told what was done for me.

Mary was fitted with a hand brace that holds her pencil and paint brush. She has learned to write and also type one key at a time with this gadget. She has gadgets for her comb, lipstick, and toothbrush and a special fork and spoon. Do you know what it is like to be fed by someone else for 12 months? Eating alone is an accomplishment itself. Of course, we cut her meat, etc. I was taught her treatments and exercises and give them to her each day. I know I have died a thousand deaths taking care of her. It is like a knife cutting through your heart to be asked to move her foot or lift her arm or turn her at night. At last you think you will become immune to the hurts, but you don't. Polio is the first thing on your mind in the morning, the last thing at night, and all during your waking hours.

I hope I haven't sounded too depressed. We still have so many things to be thankful for, and we count our many blessings. When Mary was in the iron lung, the doctors told me she would never sing again. She does, substituting some diaphragm muscles for those paralyzed in her chest. She sings in our church choir from her wheelchair, sings for weddings and funerals, and last year sang on our local radio station for a March of Dimes request program. Mary is tutored at home.

Folks ask me if I am bitter about my son's untimely death. Naturally I am human and feel my loss greatly, but I am resigned to the facts. I had a fine son, and I was privileged to have him for close to 18 years. Isn't this more than a lot of women ever have?

There are the "bad days," few and far between at our house, when the hardships do seem greater than the rewards for struggle. There are those times of heartache when feelings are stronger than courage. How do we overcome them? Our solution: just as we pray each day for our daily bread, so each day we ask God's help for courage and strength from day to day. It is surprising how little it takes to make you happy after you've had a severe bout with polio. God doesn't owe us a certain standard of living. I once read this question in an article by someone in a wheelchair, "Did you ever hear of anyone becoming famous because he could walk?" With that you come face to face with the questions of personal tragedies, the why of it all. Why do crooks, cheats, and murderers have sound limbs while a precious son, daughter, husband, or wife suffers polio or other crippling diseases? I feel my life has been enriched by polio in many ways—meeting new friends, knowing I am of very special use to those I love. The handicapped are helped mentally when they know their dear ones will not turn from them.

Her speech concluded with strong encouragement to work hard in that 1953 campaign reminding them how near they were to a victory over the dreaded disease. She again thanked everyone by restating how much the NFIP had meant to us. She never said too much about that speech. It must have torn her apart to recall it all. Somehow I think Vernon Nickell would have remembered it. Although I did not know about this copy or read it until 30 years after it was given, I was very moved by it.

Going through files of school mementoes took much more time than I expected. Sample student papers, letters from parents, copies of special projects I had developed, and news clippings took me back over those 20 years of teaching. I found the poem written directly to me by the beautiful, young black girl who was so sensitive that she found great difficulty living in the real world. Once she wrote,

You
in the wheelchair
never know
the happiness
of running across
the meadow
or the thrill
of climbing a tree
yet I envy
you
cos ('cause) you know
the <u>real</u> joys
and satisfactions
of life,
those that I
cannot find
though I search
through my mind
in the dark,
     lonely caverns...

I have never forgotten Audrey. Each year I use one of her poems in my poetry unit. Rereading her words, I wondered where she was, what had become of her. So many students had passed in and out of my life, and so many had left such vivid impressions. I recalled the shock of my first student to die. Somehow working each day with young people, I did not think often of their mortality. In the normal course of events they would all outlive me, but traffic accidents, cancer, the Vietnam War, and violent crime had been among the causes of their deaths. I wondered if I had marked their lives as positively as they had mine — especially when some of their life spans had been so short.

Sandi had taught art until she married and moved away. She had wanted a big family, but I never guessed her frustration as we corresponded superficially over the years. I had not known of her writing talents either until she wrote of the poems she was writing for her adopted daughter and sent me one she had written for me called "On Remembering."

I can remember Mary, quite contrary,
Who reached her pupils ... sitting there
Teaching from a wheelchair;
For with lifeless legs she walked with kings
And was a garden in the springtime
To anyone in the winter of their lives.

I thought her joy was complete when she and her husband adopted a second child, a boy. But it was Sandi herself in the winter of her life, and I did not recognize the signs. Nothing prepared me for the shock when I received word she had taken her life. Like everyone who has ever cared deeply about a suicide victim, I asked myself what I could have done differently, indeed, what I *should* have done. John Donne had said, "Each man's death diminshes me," but none so surely as the suicide victim's.

The days of reading and sorting were reflexive days tinged with regrets. I recalled so many good friends over the years with whom I had lost contact, yet I remembered and appreciated how much their lives had enriched mine. Why hadn't I paused more often in my daily contacts to tell people how much they meant to me, to send the words of sympathy, to say thanks?

When school started in the fall of 1980, I put the unfinished manuscript away, expecting to return to it during some of the long quiet, indoor weekends of January and February. Such was not to be the case.

During the previous school year the Board of Education had begun implementing an energy-saving program that included removing the glass from classroom windows and replacing it with insulated panels. Replacing glass during school hours was most inconvenient, but worse that the inconvenience were the noxious fumes from the panels themselves and the silicone compound used to caulk them. Although only the upstairs windows were replaced at my school, many teachers and students suffered headaches and nausea. I also suffered several asthma attacks and severe headaches.

Mr. Hulmes, my principal, retired that year. He knew of my breathing limitations and told me on the last day of school that he had submitted a memorandum requesting my classroom glass be replaced during vacation to avoid the hazard of my teaching in the foul air. "If this isn't done," he said, "and they come during school time, you let me know. I'll use whatever influence I have to stop them." He was unfailingly thoughtful.

All the first floor classrooms still had their glass windows when I began working for my new principal that fall of 1980. His dynamic energy inspired many of us to try to do better and I found areas where I had become lax and tried to improve. I enjoyed my teaching and was putting a great effort into it. The days flew past. In November I was offered the chance to write curriculum materials for Houghton Mifflin the following summer on a free lance basis. Things were going my way.

I returned from a wonderful Christmas vacation to disaster. During the recess all the first floor classroom windows had been replaced with the insulated panels. Someone in administration probably thought that timing complied with Mr. Hulmes' request. But it was winter and cold! No windows had been opened to air the building. I returned in January of 1981 to a building filled with noxious fumes. What could I do?

My first thought was of how I could cope and still fulfill my obligations to my students. My breathing was raspy and wheezy within the first hour. Dad picked me up as early as possible after school each day, but my choking spells multiplied to several a day. I escaped my classroom twice each day—for a study hall in the auditorium and for my plan period in the office where the regular windows had been left in place. With weekends to rest I thought I could make it, but I was wrong.

I began to have asthma attacks daily. One weekend I simply could not recover. My lungs had deteriorated to a point that I began to run a high fever and developed a severe respiratory infection. Our beloved family doctor had retired, but Dr. Cargill, though not as familiar with my lengthy history of breathing problems, was marvelously competent. He made a house call, as I was too sick to go to him. His first line of attack was the respiratory infection. I was to stay home from school until the temperature was down. I had never missed more than one day at a time for illness until then, but I was too sick to care and almost too sick to prepare lessons for a substitute. Had I known then that I was suffering permanent lung damage, I would have taken a month's leave of absence. Instead, I thought a week's rest would cure me.

God sent the strength for me to "hang in there," as the kids say, but it was a costly commitment. The week of spring break and warmer weather, when windows could be opened, finally helped me regain some strength. I survived somehow until school ended. Summer promised the chance to rest.

Returning to the rigors of teaching in the fall of 1981 quickly revealed the weakness in my lungs. I could no longer detect fumes in the building, yet as the year wore on, I grew weaker. A further complication arose when my favorite wheelchair became irreparable. It was the American electric wheelchair that I had purchased in 1960, the one that gave me the most sitting comfort, a restful change for my back when I came home each day. Over the years we had accumulated an extra control box, four extra motors, and assorted spare parts.

The motor manufacturer in nearby McHenry no longer made those motors and had been refusing to repair the old ones for years. I would willingly have bought new ones and always paid my repair bills promptly. The last pair had been returned barely operable, but I was willing to creep along at snail speed at home for the comfort of that chair. Once more Dad took my best two motors in person to plead for their repair. What he picked up later was just a box of loose pieces.

The wheelchairs available were not what I wanted and not comfortable. The new designs were for rugged, indoor-outdoor use that I didn't need. I was reluctant to spend $4,000 for a wheelchair that wasn't what I wanted. I rented a wheelchair temporarily. I would wait for the new models. Sitting grew more tiring, however.

Fatigue contributed to an increase in choking spells and asthma attacks. I thought if I could just make it until Christmas break, I could rest then. I knew I was not well. I had been trying to hide my discomfort and weakness from others, even my parents and perhaps myself. Yet each day my breathing grew shallower. People began to notice the quick little gasps of breath I needed to complete a sentence when I spoke. In classes I had to change the pace of my phrasing. The surest indication was the loss of my ability to sing. More than 30 years earlier, when doctors said I would never sing again, God had given me back a song, a gift I had taken too lightly. For weeks I had had trouble singing the hymns in church. As Christmas approached, I tried a few carols at home. Suddenly I was aware of the thin, feeble quality and the short, gaspy phrasing. I could no longer sing!

A fortunate change in my school schedule gave me my plan period the last thing in the day that year. I began to have to leave school early during that period as I was running out of breath. On one such day when I arrived home early, barely able to talk, Mother insisted I see the doctor. I knew she was right, but I hadn't wanted to give in. The doctor order x-rays, which showed that the curvature of my spine had deepened so as to restrict breathing. Also, my lungs had been damaged; I had emphysema. It was a jolt to realize I was old enough for emphysema and that it afflicted nonsmokers.

The doctor prescribed using an Intermittent Positive Pressure Breathing machine twice daily at home. This respirator unit exercised my restricted lungs at the same time that a mist of medication was inhaled. The machine was not uncomfortable to use, but I disliked it because it required a certain amount of maintenance, connecting and changing the hoses, measuring the medication, and washing the little resevoir. Dad cheerfully undertook all this, but I resented anything that made my care any more complicated. My parents were both getting older and didn't need their lives burdened anymore.

The respirator came just before Christmas, and I told myself it would only be temporary as I would build strength quickly. I attempted to adjust my life-style, beginning with a quiet holiday vacation. Fortunately, January in Illinois is a good time to restrict social engagements. I dropped all volunteer school committees and church activities—even church services as a month of ice settled on our area.

All might have gone well except for another board of education or administrative decision. The wooden seats in the school

156

auditorium were to be refinished. Nothing was to be sanded or scraped, but a dark stain and varnish was to be applied to a few seats each evening. The finish was some sort of polyurethane with a quick-drying agent so that the seats could be used the next day for classes and study halls, one of which was mine. I think the finish was one of those that always have a caution on the label to use in a well-ventilated room. Unfortunately, our auditorium had no windows, no fans, and no air-conditioning system.

The first seats were done the end of February, and the fumes permeated the downstairs. Despite my weeks on the breathing machine, I knew I was in for trouble when I entered the school. I was overcome with severe choking when I went to study hall in the auditorium. I had to leave school early. This time I went right to the doctor whose verdict was simiple and direct—stay home until the work is completed. I called my principal at home to tell him. He was naturally upset, as the work was scheduled for a series of consecutive nights, a few seats each night. This time I decided to put myself first, and I held firm. Since emphysema damage is irreversible, I realized I could not afford to lose more breathing capacity. But Mr. Covey is a man of action. He was back to me with the word that all work would be stopped until the spring break. I was out only three days.

Unfortunately, heavy fumes were already in the building. Dad and I could smell them as soon as we opened the outside door. A temporary schedule change was worked out with the cooperation of three other teachers and the two principals so that I was relieved of the auditorium study hall. I ignored my hall duty during the passing periods and stayed in my classroom with the door shut and a window open slightly. The room was not really cold, and most students appreciated the fresher air. By carefully marshalling my time and strength for my first priorities and with daily bronchial medication, I felt myself getting a little stronger.

I began each task by sharing it with God. If He wanted me to complete it, He would have to give me the strength to do so. I had been applying that philosophy in my teaching for some time. My first goal had been to complete 20 years of teaching, which secured a state pension for me (although I could not draw on it until age 55). I continued teaching after that because I loved the vocation. The first year I said I wanted the challenge of a new principal, the next year of a new assistant principal, the next of a new curriculum. My parents still provide my complete care, and they, naturally, are growing older. I myself am weaker. Therefore, it is all up to God. He must provide the strengths and skills for our every tomorrow. As Pastor Ross said in a sermon, there are two days we never need to worry about as we live the Christian life—yesterday and tomorrow. Our own Lord Jesus told us that indirectly when he taught us to pray,

"Give us this day our daily bread"—not weekly, not monthly, but one day at a time. Tomorrow is in God's hands.

> Because He lives, I can face tomorrow;
> Because He lives, all fear is gone;
> Because I know He holds the future,
> And life is worth the living just because He lives.

I began to sing again a little—nothing special, just trying to find enough breath to get a line out. Some time later I was asked to sing for a funeral and accepted. When I hung up the phone and told Mother what the call was about, she said, "You're not going to do it, are you?"

"Yes," I told her, "I said I would. I need to know if I can." The songs were familiar ones, and the organist stopped by our house to practice first.

When I left, Mother's farewell was a line gleaned from another Chicago Sunday Evening Club message. "Mama will be praying for you," she called.

I would not pretend it was an outstanding performance, but it was all right. I think I will be able to sing again, though on a more limited basis. This time I hope I will appreciate the gift.

I am trying to make complete trust my life-style. I share my concerns and my needs with God and then try not to worry about them. I work ahead on schoolwork, revising my materials and planning. I look forward to teaching. However, if the job begins to take all of my waking strength as it did at times during the last years, I have now promised myself to get out of teaching. I try to plan for some financial security. Of course, I plan ahead and take some thought for the morrow, but I do not worry much anymore. I refuse to waste time trying to anticipate every possible disaster and devise alternatives. Every day is a gift, a blessing. I know that all things in my future will work together for my good. The fact that life has held so much joy after the desolation of polio is proof of God's love and care provided through his earthly servants, my dear parents. He is a living God who will not forsake me. Because He lives, I can face tomorrow.